MORE PRAISE FOR
AUTISM IS NOT A LIFE SENTENCE

"Lynley Summers demonstrates that consistency in a chosen approach to overcoming Autism is extremely important. As a parent, Lynley chose an unconventional approach to conquering Autism, followed her instincts of what was best for her child, and fueled by her courage and dedication led to ultimate success."

– Jose M. Fuster, Father of Alejandro Fuster – Autistic, 7 years old

"This book is a well-written look into the heart and soul of a family dealing with Autism and refusing to accept the boundaries that diagnosis can place. As a parent of a child with Autism, I laughed and I cried and saw so much of myself and my child in this book. It also showed me that it is possible to set the bar high if you see potential in your child, and to never give up! Thanks for another viewpoint on how to reach into the Autism world and help coax them out."

– Rebecca Korzilius Lubbers, Mom of two children, Arizona representative for Unlocking Autism Power, secretary, Arizona Chapter of The Autism Society of America, member of the Arizona Autism Support Board

"I first met Jessica when she was three months old. I watched her play, and sing, and laugh, and light up when I held her … and then I watched her disappear. With the steadfast love, devotion, and perseverance of her mother, who refused to lose her, I was able to meet her again. And what a blessing it is to know her both then and now. Jessica is light to all who know her and a miracle to those who lost her. Both she and Lynley are truly blessed and are a walking, talking testament to this progressive option available to families living with Autism."

— April D. Ream, University of Central Arkansas

"Reading this book made me wish I had the years with my son back again. The book is very readable, and the concrete examples will be helpful to others facing some of the same issues with their children! Jessica's insights are invaluable – all too often we have very little idea of the kid's point of view, and what is happening inside – and that's where it all is! Above all, Lynley Summers sets a fine example of persistence for other parents. In every case I have heard of where people are living successfully with Autism, it is parental persistence that was the overriding success factor. Your never-give-up attitude will be an inspiration to parents everywhere. Raising a child with Autism is a sometimes wonderful, but often exhausting and exasperating, road to travel. Reading about your journey will help people keep sight of their destination. Jessica is very fortunate to have you as her mom, and all of us are very fortunate to have you both share your story."

— Carolyn Jackson, Flaghouse Inc.

"The fondest memories I have of Jessica was the way she and her mother communicated with each other, sometimes without even using words. I watched this 3-year-old evolve from a babbling, frightened and withdrawn child into a beautiful, confident, extremely intelligent young lady with no limitations. I will not say that it is a miracle because that would be unfair to the person who is responsible for her amazing journey: her mother. Jessica is a very fortunate young lady to have a mother that was and still is so dedicated to helping others see a 'silver lining' to what can be a very dark cloud. I feel blessed to have witnessed the transformation of that precious child and know that she is in the public eye sharing their story and giving other families hope. It makes me very proud to call her friend."

–Candi Wagoner, former therapy team member, Director of Children's Ministries, Richland, Mississippi

"Jessica was an active, beautiful infant. She was the center of attention in the room. Then one day, she was gone. I watched as this beautiful baby girl began to flail, bang her head, lose her ability to speak, communicate and completely shut down. I also watched as her mother refused to accept that her baby girl would spend the rest of her life in a self-contained environment, unable to communicate. Autism does not have to be a life sentence. Lynley and Jessica Summers are living proof of this, and I am proud to be a close member of this family as Jessica's godmother and team."

–Robyn A. Koch, BS, CPCS, CPMSM, Director of Continuing Education, Arkansas Pharmacists Association

"An enlightening read for anyone trying to understand the inside world of Autism from the outside. I will definitely be recommending this book to friends who work as healthcare professionals and to anyone who would like to enter the world of a child living with Autism in order to help them and us to appreciate the gifts that are locked inside. I am proud of Lynley and Jessica and what they have achieved together. They are a lesson to us all that love manifests itself in so many ways."

– Gail Armistead, LLB, United Kingdom

"I loved this book. It's such an uplifting and hopeful story. As the mother of an Asperger's child, so many of Jazz's stories were similar to what we went through with Amy. As a person who talks with other parents to help them understand their children, this will definitely be a story I want them to read. Hearing Jazz's words really helps to clarify what's going on with the kids. She is speaking for the many children who haven't yet found their 'own voice.' Parental instinct is crucial, fight for what you believe is there."

– Christa Young, Parent and advocate

"I read this book and thought it is wonderful. I can find so many things that I relate to. My diagnosis is Asperger's, and while it's a   little higher on the Autistic scale, a lot of things are the same. This book helped me find explanations for things I didn't have words for myself. I can't thank Lynley Summers enough for sharing her own and Jazz's experiences like this. It helps more people to understand what goes on in our heads and lets us know that just because we aren't typical, doesn't mean we are useless."

– Amy Young, age 17

"As an infant, Jessica came to my house. She would laugh, play and watch Disney Sing Along Song videos, swaying to the beat of the music. Then one day she was gone! She would flail, cry, beat her head and allow no one to touch her. Through the perseverance of her mother, she re-emerged. We were told that Jessica would never speak and at best she would be in a helmet in a self-contained classroom. Today, she is in high school and an honor student. At one time, college was a dream, now, it is a realistic expectation."

– Shirley Lynch, Retired Teacher, Pine Forest
Elementary, Maumelle, Arkansas

Autism Is Not
a Life Sentence

Autism Is Not a Life Sentence

How One Family Took on Autism and WON!

Lynley Summers

With Commentary by Jessica "Jazz" Summers

Foreword by Stephen Shore

Autism Asperger Publishing Co.
P.O. Box 23173
Shawnee Mission, Kansas 66283-0173
www.asperger.net

© 2006 by Autism
Asperger Publishing Co.
P.O. Box 23173
Shawnee Mission, Kansas 66283-0173
www.asperger.net

The use of selected references from various sources does not necessarily imply publisher endorsement of the versions in their entirety.

PUBLISHER'S CATALOGING-IN-PUBLICATION

Summers, Lynley.

    Autism is not a life sentence : how one family took on autism and won! / Lynley Summers ; with commentary by Jessica "Jazz" Summers ; foreword by Stephen Shore. – 1st ed. – Shawnee Mission, Kan. : Autism Asperger Pub. Co., 2006.

        p. ; cm.

      ISBN-13: 978-1-931282-88-8
      ISBN-10: 1-931282-88-9
      LCCN: 2005905904
      Includes bibliographical references and glossary.

        1. Summers, Jessica–Health. 2. Autism in children–Treatment. 3. Autistic children–Behavior modification. 4. Self-acceptance. I. Summers, Jessica. II. Title.

RJ506.A9 S86 2006   2005905904
618.92/85882–dc22   0601

Hooked on Phonics is a registered trademark of HOP, LLC, a division of Educate, Inc. Reference to the Hooked on Phonics product by the author and her portrayal of its effectiveness with her daughter's verbal development is based on personal experience and is not an endorsement or recommendation by HOP, LLC of the product for use with persons with disabilities.

Cover art: Dan Fenwick, comic book artist and enthusiast, has contributed to such publications as the *Auburndale Sun* and Tampa, Florida's *Weekly Planet*. *Autism Is Not a Life Sentence* is his first book cover illustration. *Shreds of Humanity*, his independent comic book series, is forthcoming. He lives in Brooklyn, New York.

This book is designed in Times New Roman and Frutiger Condensed.

Printed in the United States of America.

Acknowledgments

To my family: Steve, Jazz, Alex and Averie. Without your support and understanding, your patience, and the nights you were willing to eat Spaghettios, we would never have gotten to the finish line on this project! Mom loves you guys!

My gratitude goes to my MeeMaw, for helping make the project possible from the beginning, and for helping to get us to convention! Thank you to Keith Myles, to Brenda Myles, and to my incredible editor, Kirsten McBride, and the wonderful team at AAPC for their tireless efforts.

Thanks a million to the "Million Dollar Woman!," Bobbi McKenna, and her Book Club for Authors for teaching me all the right ways to take the parts of story and a disjointed dissertation and turn it into a book. Your model really works, Bobbi!

Many thanks to my good friend Stephen Shore, for encouraging me throughout the project, and for writing the foreword. I am also flapping and spinning very much over the fact that he only calls me on days that have the letter "T" in them.

This book project is possible due in part to the managerial and editorial efforts of Mr. Matt Dozier. He is a life-long friend and a former instructor of composition and literature. He is currently the national director of an educational non-profit based in Little Rock, Arkansas. Matt Dozier is the kind of person that let me send the manuscript to him nine or ten times without threatening to hate me, and helped me to make all the right changes to get it ready. He also sent emails to keep me on track because he realized that there were others out there like me who needed this book. He recognized my vision. This book would absolutely, positively, not be in your hands without his efforts. Thank you, Mr. Dozier.

This project would not have been possible without the efforts of the people who were involved, whether by acting on the therapy team, serving as focus group members or by otherwise collaborating to produce this work. I am in your debt:

Lisa Craver, Linda Hampton, April Ream, Robyn, Dan & Jonathan Reese Koch, Dr. Tony Attwood, Dr. Liane Holliday Willey, Carolyn Jackson, Flaghouse, Inc., David, Christa & Amy Young, Linda and Jack Walker, Dr. Michael & Karen Potts, Shirley & Lloyd Lynch, Susan Perry Simpson, Jose Fuster, Gail Armistead, Robert & Pam Russell, TEACCH, Candice Wagoner, Rebecca K. Lubbers, the UT Medical Group-Memphis, Tennessee, Dr. Gayle Woodson, LeBonheur Children's Medical System, Mills University Studies High School, Mr. Bill Barnes, Northwood Middle School, Immaculate Heart of Mary School, Itoi Elementary School-Wadayama, Japan, College Lakes Elementary, Mr. Sheldon Harvey, Long Hill Elementary, Ms. Donna Albaugh, Alma Easom Elementary, Ms. Connie Graham, The Guy School, Mr. Sam Guy, Brentwood Elementary School, Ms. Karen Roberts, Dr. Kay Stuart, Ms. Fran Salisbury, the Hooked on Phonics folks, Dr. Dorothy Taguchi-Director of Editorial and Business Affairs, and Mr. Chip Paucek. Many, many thanks for the wonderful help and support of the legal team at Friday, Eldredge & Clark, in particular to Mr. Price Gardner and Mr. Robert Smith. Finally, a special thanks goes to Jerry Davis and Jerry Davis Photography for the amazing photo shoot, and to Jane White and Jane White Cosmetics for the makeup and hair for our photo session!! There are none better than these to work with! Jazz and I lucked out to get them for our pictures.

Many thanks from the Summers fam to the following, for your support and encouragement throughout this project. We couldn't have done it without you! Our parents and grandparents, sisters and brothers and extended families – thanks so much! Arkansas Disability Coalition, Wanda Stovall, Lynne McAllester, Autism Society of America, Cathy Pratt, EdD, Jeff Sell, Esq., Jim Ball, PhD, Wes Hampton, Brittany Lauren Hampton, Tyler Clay Hampton, Wilma Lea, Andy Anders,

Christy Wallace, Daisy Stringer, Arkansas Medical Care Advisory Committee, Patsy Wallace, Mr. Lee Russell, Steve & Breanna Eneberg, Angie Caramanno Frye, Danielle Dombrowski, Kim & Dwayne Nelson, Nancy Cale, Unlocking Autism, Shelley Hendrix Reynolds, Dan Marino & The Dan Marino Foundation, Doug Bartel, Marilee Thomason, Cindy Ford, Sally Landau, Mr. Yoshiya Yoshida, Mr. Toshihiro Morishita, Ms. Ryoko Hirayama, Ms. Satomi Goto Matui, Chan Weber, First Christian Church of Sherwood, AR, Will & Martha Feland, "Uncle Bob" White, the 53rd Airlift Squadron-Blackjacks and the 314 OG/GCC at Little Rock Air Force Base.

My Methodist College family: Dr. Elton Hendricks, Lynn "my Fayetteville Mom" Clark and Sam Clark, "Uncle Bill" Lowdermilk (who hired me), Mr. & Mrs. Alan Porter, Dr. & Mrs. Bob Christian, Dr. & Mrs. Robert Perkins, Dr. Anthony J. & Mrs. Pat DeLapa (Tony was the academic dean, and allowed me to drop everything and go to Jazz when she needed me at school – and allowed me to bring her back with me into my office, after hours, to keep things running smoothly. He understood our plight, and I am in his debt forever!). Dr. John Sill, Dr. Diane Guthrie, Mrs. Jane Gardiner, Gene Clayton, Carrie Parrish, Ben Wells, Jane Cherry, George Blanc, Kim Dowd, Bonnie Adamson, Shasta Culbreth, Trish Douthit, Dr. Don Lassiter, Doug Little, Nona Fisher, Bill Billings, Mike Sinkovitz, Candice Moody, Gerri Williams, Linda Gravitt, Earleene Bass, Betty Neill Parsons, Silvana Foti, Shelia Mattingly, Rick Rode, Cliff Wells, Summer Brock, Ed Cohn, Mason Sykes, Michael Colonnese, Robin Greene, Dr. Narenda Singh, Dr. Joan Bitterman, William Walker, Dr. John Campbell, Beth Elmore Butler, Kelly and David Norman, Gayle O'Brien, Joe Swanner, Carolyn Barbour, Dr. Darl Champion, Darlene Hopkins, Wilford Saunders, Dr. Paul Wilson, Dr. Mary Kirchner, Peggy Hinson, Jim Hogge, Dr. Richard and Jennifer Rohrer-Walsh, Dr. Peter Murray, Wanda Foster, Dottie Earwood, Dr. Lloyd Bailey, the biologists who let me sound my feeble ideas off them from time to time (and cry in their offices – Dr. Margaret Folsom, Dr. Lori Brookman, Dr. Linda Sue Barnes,) Nicolette Campos, Dr. Elizabeth Belford, Dr. Gillie Benstead (who told me that I should write this all down and keep going with Jessica because she, too, saw her spark!), Dr. Juanita Heyward, Dr. Wenda Johnson, Ron Foster, and Ms. Helen Matthews – who with her students gave Jessica a series of educational diagnostics to help me keep up with her progress, and who shared my vision for her.

This list is incomplete, because in my mind I can just walk the campus and go through each building and count the faces from my memory, and remember how each had helped us along our journey. As I walked through my memory and made this list, these were the faces that I saw. I often dream about Methodist College. It's a fantastic place to live and learn and to be. I am proud of the time I spent there, both as a student and as an administrator. There are many other names that should be here that I haven't the room for, and I must send this tonight so we can go to press. There are many, many more names to put on this list.

My final words of thanks go to you, the readers, the teachers, the clinicians and professionals and doctors, and to the parents of all the kids out there on the Spectrum. You are heroes, every last one of you. Keep getting up and breathing in and out every day, and having a vision for your kids of something better. The sun is going to go down today, and it's going to come up again tomorrow. What you do with the day is up to you. Everything is therapy. Thank you for letting me share mine with you.

Lynley Summers

Dedication

This book is dedicated to four strong women in my life. I have to start this list with my great-grandmother. I called her Mamaw. She departed this life when I was 15 years old. Please take a voyage with me into my memory banks now, so that I may introduce you.

I am standing next to my great-grandmother and I am a little girl. We are cooking. Okay, SHE is cooking. She is teaching me how to cook. Mamaw is about 5 feet tall, blue-haired and delicately built. She embodies dignity, integrity, hope, and faith. She has a bright smile; she is charming, and I love her dearly. She plays cards with me and teaches me about flowers, especially roses, which she grows in a garden outside her back door. She tells me stories about her family; about life when she was a girl, about love and about losing love. She is very wise. She talks about her children a lot. She talks to me because lots of other people are too busy to listen to a woman in her eighties. I love to listen to my Mamaw. She listens to me play the piano and sing almost every day we are together. Sometimes she tries to teach me how to cook. Like this day.

She does funny things sometimes. For example, she measures flour by the handfuls. Her hands are really small like mine. It's pretty easy, but my MeeMaw (her daughter, my grandmother) reminds me that I will have to change the recipe when my hands start to grow bigger. I have to memorize how big the piles of salt or sugar are in the palm of my hand, or remember to use the special spoon from the drawer. My mom has some cups with lines and measurements on them, I tell Mamaw. She just purses her lips and says those things are too complicated. She tells me to learn how to do it right – then I never need to keep up with any of those other things.

We are sitting next to two different pots. One is full of stuff just bubbling away, the other is right in front of us, needing to be stirred every second. They are for the same recipe. I am confused. Both pots have the same ingredients in them. Mamaw says it's tricky sometimes. Some pots have to be watched a little more than others. They need stirring so the sugar doesn't stick to the bottom, or you have to throw out the whole batch. "Lynley, if you just take the time to stir it right, it's fine. Some people are like that, too," she adds. "Two people in the same room or in the same class together," she says. "One might be fine left alone, like that pot over there. But this one here needs to be stirred up all the time or it's just no good."

Did I say she was teaching me how to cook? No, she was teaching me how to treat people, how to live my life. Many years later, I would hear her words echoing in my heart as I kept hovering over my daughter, stirring her ...

Let's come back to the present day, and to the list of strong women in my life. The second woman on the list has already been mentioned, my MeeMaw. MeeMaw remains to this day my moral compass. There are no words to adequately describe the devotion to family that MeeMaw has instilled in us all. The thing that strikes me most about my MeeMaw is her smile. She lights up a whole room. When you look at her wedding portrait, taken more than 60 years ago, you see the same smile. A great deal has happened to shake her during the intervening time, but she has retained that gentleness. She has kept her light. Her love and support has been a beacon guiding me through many rough seas, and her faith and strength has inspired me every day of my life. If I ever grow up, she is who I want to be.

The third woman is my mother. Continuing the line of strong females in my family, my mother led by example. She gave me the model for a strong work ethic. She has also completely mastered all the skills of making kids feel loved and special. Besides, Mom's got great attention to detail. She gave me a good model to follow. Aside from teaching me right from wrong, she taught me how to respect others, and laid a foundation of sound, loving discipline. If any of my rules make sense, then the groundwork was laid in my childhood in her home. When Jessica was diagnosed, though we were over a thousand miles away, Mom read everything she possibly could on Autism to try to understand how we could help Jessica. At a time when I felt most alone, that helped me tremendously.

The fourth woman on the list is still a woman-in-training. To my daughter, Jessica (I call her Jazz): Since the moment I knew you were coming, I wanted to be your mom. If I could pick any child in the universe to be mine, I would pick you. You are perfect the way you are, and you always have been. You can do whatever you make up your mind to do. Go for it, girlie!

Jazz and I have grown so much together over the last 10 years. Without her, believing and trusting in me, I would never have survived. In many ways, one might say we saved each other. She continues to teach me. Most of her lessons deal with courage. I thought that I knew about being brave, but Jazz takes it to totally new heights. It is thrilling to watch her grow into such a bright and brilliant young woman.

I am proud to be a link in this family chain: my Mamaw, my MeeMaw, my Mom, me, and my Jessica. I have been greatly blessed. MeeMaw taught me a saying when I was 17 years old: "To whom much is given, much is expected ..." She was right. There is no way to repay the debt I owe. This dedication, and my unwavering devotion, will have to suffice until I can think of something better.

All my love,

Lynley Aileen Summers

Table of Contents

Foreword

Drawing strength from a legacy of powerful women in her life, Lynley launches the reader on a rollercoaster ride of her family's struggle to teach her daughter, Jessica, who was diagnosed with Autism how to not only live, but to prosper. The story opens with a discussion of certain pots of food needing "to be stirred up all the time" between Lynley's and her wise great-grandmother. Many years later, the concept of "stirring up the pot" was to play a major role in Lynley's and, ultimately, Jessica's success.

Hit with the "Autism bomb" at 19 months, Jessica was initially pronounced by professionals as material for special education and wearing a helmet to prevent self-abusive behaviors with a trajectory likely to land her in a sheltered workshop and living in an institution. However, as you read through this journey, Jessica is now blasting her way through high school, composing music, writing stories, and speaking at conferences about life with Autism.

Beginning with the principles of applied behavioral analysis, this newly minted student of Autism realizes much more is needed for Jessica's success. First, Lynley educates the reader as she assimilates everything possible about how sensory differences, literal thought, cognitive functioning, and other characteristics of Autism play a vital role in how Jessica perceives, interprets, and finally interacts with her environment. Harkening back to her great-grandmother's directive of "stirring the pot," in a stroke of genius, Lynley mixes her doctoral studies on chaos theory into the stew that becomes Jessica's early intervention program.

Lynley tackles the challenge of educating her daughter with the fervor of a scientist conducting a Nobel Prize-winning study. From knockdown, hair-pulling battles in front of astonished onlookers to Jessica's writings of what life was like for her during these trying times, you will bear witness to the power of a mother's love and determination as – through one change in routine at a time – she transforms her daughter's existence of chaos to a life of order, connectedness, and opportunity.

Although having a child with Autism may seem like a tragedy to many people, Lynley not only perseveres to give Jessica the tools she needs to live a fulfilling and productive life, she also comes to the realization that Autism has been a blessing that allowed her to develop a much closer bond with her child than would otherwise have been.

Upon finishing Lynley and Jessica's story, the reader will know how one mother-daughter team worked together to build a life of fulfillment and success – not by beating Autism, but by working with it. Although the book comes to an end, the story continues. Lynley is proud of her daughter beyond words and truly believes that her daughter is perfect just the way she is. We will hear a lot more from this amazing team in the days to come.

Stephen Shore, 20 March, 2005
Brookline, Massachusetts
Doctoral candidate in special education, Boston University
Author of *Beyond the Wall: Personal Experiences with Autism and Asperger Syndrome*
Editor/co-author, *Ask and Tell: Self-Advocacy and Disclosure for People on the Autism Spectrum*
Board President of the Asperger's Association of New England

Introduction

"Meet the Folks, Kick off Your Shoes and Sit a Spell"

All families deal with a tremendous amount of stress when raising children, but when a child has a pervasive developmental disorder like one on the Autism Spectrum, the stress is immeasurably magnified. There is ever-present grief for a while: You should be able to socialize but you can't as it may upset your child's need for sameness and routine. You shouldn't dread the ringing of the phone. The phone is something that you can't schedule. What if a neighbor should drop by your house and ring the doorbell? This sound alone could trigger an episode. Visits from out-of-town family members bring more stress than just cleaning the bathroom and putting out the guest towels. The grandparents would love to spoil their granddaughter, but she won't let them even hug her. The looks on their faces break your heart. Your mind screams, "What kind of a daughter are you?" The teacher asks you to stay after school to help explain why your child runs shrieking from the room. The look on the teacher's face is stern and confused, asking "What kind of a mother are you?" Your husband would love a sweet "daddy's little girl," but he can't. Your heart aches. What did you do wrong? Your aunt comes laden with gifts for her great-niece, but your child looks past her, humming to herself, totally unresponsive, then screams and strikes your aunt in the face and cries out. Nobody understands that it's a really bad day for her. Maybe the next day will be okay and she'll be fine, but who knows? You suffer all kinds of guilt constantly.

And it does not stop at the end of the day. Your anguish causes you to drop in sheer exhaustion into restless sleep. Your nightmares are full of vivid images of what you endure all day long, and your thoughts wander during the waking hours to include a list of horrible things that might befall your child if you were to become ill, or worse yet, if you DIED – "What would become of her? Who would care for her? She would be lost ... lost ... LOST!!!" There is no respite and no retreat. When the days are long and hard, and the load seems particularly heavy, there is nobody to pick up the slack.

That's not to say that every day was a bad day for Jessica. She did have days that were manageable, but we dealt with Autism every single day of our lives, in everything that we did. And since there is no cure, we will deal with it for the rest of our lives. And that's okay with us.

Dealing with the initial grief was difficult. I never wished for my daughter to be the first woman elected president of the United States; I never hoped for her to be a Nobel Prize-winning astrophysicist; I never dreamed for her to win an Oscar, or a Grammy, or an ANYTHING in particular. I simply wanted, and still want, for my daughter to have a life of her own. I want her to have success in the areas where she excels, mixed with enough failure to keep her humble and hard working. I want her to have her heart broken at least once, because it means that she will love. I want her to know true joy, but that means she must understand sacrifice and loss. I want her to be comfortable in her skin, and to see herself as the beautiful creature that she is, with her many gifts and talents, and that she is perfect the way she was created, with Autism. I want her to be able to care for herself, to be proud of her accomplishments, and proud of her failings – perhaps because they will show her how she has grown. I want her to have ownership in a life that has worth and meaning to her, and to be able to share that life with others who surround her with support and love. I want what most parents should want.

It is with great pleasure that I welcome you into our life, to show you our world. We are blessed by Autism. Years ago, you would probably not have heard me say this; however, through the course of my journey with Jessica, I have come to many realizations. One of those realizations is that your perception of where you are is the key to your sense of well-being. I perceive that we are blessed by Autism.

My daughter and I have come to know one another well. We trust each other. We read each other's signals. We anticipate one another. We know each other's nonverbal cues. We are closer than most moms and daughters. We have Autism to thank for this. I didn't have the luxury of being able to say "I'll get to that in a minute, honey," or to use the TV as a babysitter. I had to know what Jessica was watching on TV, so I watched everything with her. I explained every tiny detail. With something like Autism, you take nothing for granted. That is, you should never assume that persons with Autism know what is being discussed, or have tapped into their personal store of experiential knowledge, or that they can perceive differences in the emotional states of others, such as characters in a play. They are able to learn to do these things, but often they don't notice significant clues to lead them to draw the correct conclusions without help and support. It can be very tedious, but patient guidance yields great rewards.

It still is very tedious at times, because although Jessica has progressed at miraculous rates, and can function at a level that far surpasses anything her original prognosis suggested, we must continue to work constantly.

This book is our story. It is the story of how Jessica descended into darkness from what appeared to be a normal infancy. It tells of how I incorporated chaos theory into behavioral modification therapy, and used it successfully to systematically eliminate some of the characteristically Autistic behaviors from Jessica's life. She once flapped and rocked and spun objects, and had problems making eye contact. I had to worry about her walking off the end of docks into the lake, or into traffic because she had no fear of danger. These behaviors are in the past. She understands the environment around her now. The child that I lost to The Void, that I mourned, for fear that we would not be able to connect or communicate, now considers me to be her best friend. We are blessed with a close and loving relationship, full of love and laughter.

Jessica is a miracle. When she was diagnosed at age 4, she was a rocking, spinning, head-banging, shrieking, flailing, not-ready-for-the-public-kind-of-child. Two speech therapists told me that she would not communicate in English and that I should not expect her to do so. We were looking at self-contained special education classrooms – in a helmet – with the hope of a high school equivalency diploma by the age of 21. After that, she would likely be living in a some social group or institutional-type setting as an adult. College would be out of the question.

Our journey has not been an easy one. Jessica will soon celebrate her 16th birthday. We have been hard at work for more than 10 years. Jessica likes to be called "Jazz" because there are too many Jessicas. I'm afraid that I started it when she was a baby, but it only recently caught on as we have continued to work on humor, which is often a foreign concept to the Autistic mind. She discovered that it was funny, and somewhat cool, to have a nickname that sets you apart, and "Jazz" really does suit her. I mention this as an aside, because it is uncommon for Autistic kids to take a nickname. Many are uncomfortable shortening their first names, for instance, from Robert to "Rob," or Michael to "Mike." They don't like it, on general principle, even if the person giving them the nickname is doing so out of fondness for them. The person with Autism might not be able to accept it because there is the mental stumbling block of the nickname in the way. Thus, for Jessica to pick a nickname like "Jazz" was a milestone socially.

That sounds pretty normal for such an allegedly abnormal child, doesn't it? Well, listen to this: She is currently in the 11th grade, having skipped the 6th altogether. She attends Mills University Studies High School in Little Rock Arkansas, ranked #20 in the nation by *Newsweek*. Not only does she speak English beautifully, she is fully functional in Japanese as well. She composes her own piano music, and has a beautiful singing voice. She tried out for All-Region Choir, and last year she placed among the highest in the central region in Arkansas and was chosen as the outstanding sophomore choir member. In her freshman year of high school, she won a departmental award for science and technology and was the outstanding freshman choir member.

She writes her own stories, and is a gifted artist, drawing and painting in manga, or Japanese comic book style. She won her school's only art award in the 8th grade, and was selected as one of eight young artists whose work was displayed on buildings around town. She got to direct a team of artists for that project. She is even a member of Bobbi McKenna's Book Club for Authors, which is a program for adults. Not bad for a kid who was never supposed to communicate in English at all!

In short, she does things that Autistic children are often unable to do because of the limitations of the disorder. We continue to work to remove those limitations, and she continues to improve. She is fully mainstreamed at school, both academically and socially. College is expected. She can do whatever she wants, just like everyone else.

I have always been honest with Jessica. I felt that it was important that she know the truth about her condition. Even though she was only 4 years old when we received her diagnosis, I didn't shield her from the adult talk. In fact, I encouraged her to listen to it. When she was finding her voice, I began talking to her about Autism, and what it meant to have Autism. It meant that she was very special. It meant that her mind might work differently than mine did, so we had to be patient with each other. Since the moment when she found the right words to ask, she has been full of questions about everything. Some of her questions have not been easy to answer!

As anyone will tell you who has an individual in the house who is on the Autism Spectrum, that individual misses nothing. It isn't unusual for a child on the spectrum to look at you from the corner of his eye and ask, in his loudest outdoor voice, within earshot of Aunt Edna, why you just tossed your piece of Aunt Edna's cake into the trash can? You have to stop right then and explain. You have to give him an answer right away. He will not be ignored.

Jessica knew from about age 6 that she had Autism, and she understood to the extent a 6-year-old can what it meant to be Autistic. I had to educate myself about all the ways Autism affects the brain and how it affects the processing of information. Then it was my job to pass my learning onto Jessica in a positive and constructive way. I knew that attitude would be the key to unleashing and nurturing her full potential. Perception is the key. I told her that it was important that she understand that some kids have freckles because they have sensitive skin. Some kids wear eyeglasses because their eyes don't work like yours and mine do. Some kids have blond hair and some have black hair. Some have Autism, and some kids are afraid of the dark; some use wheelchairs, some have legs that work just fine; some kids like grape jelly and others don't like jelly at all with their peanut butter – that's just the way it is. It's neither good nor bad.

She listened and took all this in, and then nodded. It made sense to us both. As long as we didn't make a big deal out of it, then it shouldn't BE a big deal. The main point that I made to Jessica was that having Autism was an explanation for why things seemed out of place to her sometimes or why she might feel out of control at times, but never, ever, was it to be used as an excuse for why she couldn't do something. If anything, it should be the opposite. We used Autism to motivate her. She and I agreed that Autism or not, she wouldn't limit herself.

Jessica will tell you that the angriest she has ever seen me was one time when she was particularly lazy (imagine a kid being lazy)! Jessica asked if she could have her snack before lunchtime. We were hiking, and I told her that she would be allowed to have her snack after lunch, and that she was expected to remain with the group until that time. She either didn't listen to the answer or she didn't like the answer, for she was soon found eating her snack at the end of the line. When she realized how angry her behavior made me, she remarked to her Godmother that she didn't understand what I had instructed her to do, because she was Autistic. In 10 years, this is the only example I can think of when Jessica has tried to use Autism as an excuse. In fact, it was so unusual that it shocked all three of us to the core. There was no screaming, as I rarely raise my voice. There were some tears though; mostly hers. After full realization had settled in, she couldn't believe what she had said. It stands as a testament to the dedication that we all, as a team, have to furthering her therapy!

But that wasn't Autism. That was "kid." She'd figured out how to work it. She has never tried to use it again, and I doubt she ever would.

Understanding that you have Autism, or that a loved one has Autism, and understanding Autism itself are very different things. There are many things about Autism that Jessica and I do not understand. There are many things that the "experts" don't understand. Because Autism has played such a large role in our lives, I capitalize the word, even though technically it shouldn't be capitalized.

I will attempt to give a brief overview, in layman's terms, of what Autism is, how it manifests itself, and also let you know where you can find more information on the subject. There are a lot of theories; new information about Autism surfaces all the time. It is a lifelong disorder for which there is presently no cure.

If you share Autism with us, perhaps you will find some ground on which to stand. Families don't always recognize that they have options, and instead find themselves stuck in a schedule, a routine, a rut, that slowly edges out all those things that they would like to be doing with their families and friends.

Right here at the very beginning, I want to talk about one of the most serious side effects of living with Autism: caregiver stress. These words apply to any situation where a family member requires special care and undivided attention. When Autism is part of the mix, caregiver stress is taken to a whole new level, because there seem to be no outlets, no escapes, no reprieves. It seems like nobody in the outside world understands the predicament of the caregiver. To others, it often seems that you simply have a discipline problem; that your child is out of control. To an employer, you may be seen as unreliable. To a physician, you are a zealot. To a teacher, you are a nuisance. To neighbors, you are a hermit.

Living with a person who has severe Autism sometimes means that if something unexpected pops up, you won't be able to take part. That is, life goes on outside your world, but you cannot attend parties, showers, weddings or funerals because they are not part of the regular routine. If you become ill or need to pick up something from the grocery or the drugstore, forget it. If a serious storm front is coming, expect another one inside your home as well. Forget visiting the sick or infirm; forget volunteer work, church work, or anything spontaneous; forget anything outside the safety zone of the routine. Nothing exists outside the routine. A life like this for the caregiver can be a prison of sorts, and can seem to be a life sentence.

But I will show you that there are options. It will take work and commitment, but the rewards are great. It wasn't easy to get where Jessica and I are today. Spurred by Jessica's condition, I have devoted my life to behavioral science, and now work with kids and adults across the spectrum. Now that Jessica and I have liberated ourselves from "what might have been," I see my job as sharing what we did so that other kids, like Jessica, and other parents, like me, can use the techniques that we used.

I wrote this book in part due to Jessica's prompting. For many years, we have shared our story with parents and families all around the country. Jessica is functioning at a level where she can choose to disclose information about Autism when and if she wants to do so. She feels a strong sense of duty to others on the Autism Spectrum, as do I, and she asked me one day to write it all down because there were so many others out there who may need it. In addition, she has chosen to contribute her own words to several of the chapters. I never prompted her, or pushed her. I let her read the manuscript as I was writing it, and where she felt led to chime in, she did so. She has a lot of stories regarding her therapy that are probably better aimed at kids and teens, so she is working on a book of her own. I am touched every day by her courage and her willingness to share her story, and to extend a hand to others on the same journey. She is fearless.

Finally, it is important to remember that what works for one child may not work for another. Many parents are looking to read everything, and will try anything, to help their child. But many begin to lose hope once their spectrum child gets past the critical "early intervention" age. I have had great success with these same techniques, in much older children. I didn't begin with my stepson Averie until he was 8 years old. I began working with him the day that we met. He has made tremendous strides. In addition, I have seen marked improvement after only two weeks in an 18-year-old young man who began using the program outlined here with his parents.

Many parents will have time restraints, but certainly there are ways that families can see improvements that can help make their lives better. Improvement is improvement. Don't give up! I ask you the questions that I asked myself: What is there to lose in trying? What have you to gain? What has your child to gain?

Autism touches more than the immediate family. Aunts and uncles, cousins, teachers, friends, neighbors, church families, coaches, and health professionals working in the field are all touched by it. Jessica and I hope that you can take something you need from her story. We hope that it will inspire, uplift and energize you. More than that, we offer you our proven techniques in the hope that you may replicate our miracle.

Jessica Speaks: On Autism

The first time my mom told me I was Autistic was when I was 6. At first, I considered it to be some sort of curse, like a hex from a witch or something. Then again, I was into fantasy stories at the time. I don't see it as a curse today. I consider it a gift.

I remember that it was rough for me and my mom when I was little. To be perfectly honest, I must have been a real pain. But the only thing I can say is that I didn't know what I was doing. I thought what I was doing was natural.

I thought that other people knew what I was going through, and that they knew what I was thinking. In reality, they didn't. I remember a time when I thought that everybody knew who my mom was, and who my family was, and what was in my mind.

I used to think that I was a freak because I was Autistic. I thought people would hate me because I was different. That scared me. Now I know better. I know that there is no such thing as freaks. Well, actually, there are freaks. Freaks are the people who call other people freaks. Since I have a family and many friends who love me very much, it doesn't matter that I am Autistic. I have a place where I belong. That's all that matters.

CHAPTER ONE

What Is Autism?

"Breaking It Down for Everyone to Understand"

Think for a moment about how different all the many forms of cancer are. Cancers of the ovaries, the bones, and the blood ... three different scenarios. Three different stories. The treatments are different, the outcomes are different, and the prognosis in each case may be quite different. The success rate of each may also be dramatically different. And yet, they are all cancers.

Autism also comes in many forms. We have all heard cancer referred to as "The Big C" at one time or another. I call Autism "The Big A" for that very reason. Please don't misunderstand me. I don't see Autism as a cancer in our society, or as a cancer in our family. Quite the opposite; as already mentioned, I see it as a blessing. Everything that you survive, that you overcome is a blessing. Cancer survivors will tell you something similar. Experiences like this put everything in your life into sharp perspective in a hurry. I speak the word with pride, and I speak of the last decade with pride in my daughter, for the hard work and effort that she continues to put forth.

Nobody knows what causes Autism. The first thing that people usually ask me relates to the cause. I didn't smoke or drink anything unusual, nor was I exposed to lead paint chips or asbestos during my pregnancy. I didn't fall down a flight of steps or anything like that with Jessica when she was an infant. I didn't ignore her, or fail to interact with her in her formative years, as was commonly thought to be a cause back in the days when Autism was referred to as childhood schizophrenia. There is nothing to point my finger at and place the blame upon, which is what many parents want to do, as knowing a specific cause can make it easier to cope.

Autism is a neurological disorder, and is often described as a complex developmental disability. It usually appears during the first three years of life. Four out of five individuals with Autism are boys. It affects the normal development of the brain in the areas of communication and social interaction in general. When Jessica was diagnosed in 1994, the Centers for Disease Control and Prevention, or CDC, estimated that Autism occurred for every 1 in 10,000 births. That number now, 10 years later, is 1 in 166 births.

It is important to recognize that we know a great deal more now than we ever did about Autism. The proper diagnosis at the earliest possible stage of development is crucial. More effective diagnostics may be part of the cause of the higher numbers. That is, the number may be slightly skewed due to more accurate reporting. However, there is a higher incidence of the disorder, and a much higher number of individuals on the spectrum today than ever before.

A spectrum disorder means that the symptoms and characteristics can present themselves across a wide pattern, or spectrum, in any combination from mild to severe. So, if you have two people with the very same "form" of Autism, they may act very differently from one another and have various skill levels. They are very likely to have varying behaviors as well.

There are commonalities within the disorder, and there are common misconceptions. I will attempt to deal with both at once. I believe that The Autism Society of America, or ASA, is the best resource available for anyone who is interested in learning the basics about Autism, and I am on their website (www.autism-society.org) several times each week, reading the latest that research has to offer our community. For the purpose of writing this chapter, I went there to get the most current information. I'll start with the listing that they provided for common Autistic traits, and then add my own notes. These are in the same order that you would find them on the ASA site.

Insistence on sameness; resistance to change

This resistance to change is directly related to the main theme of this book, and the main focus of my work. The tendency among individuals with Autism is to resort to a schedule, often a rigorous, tedious one. This can become a prison term of sorts for the caregiver, or for siblings or other family members living in the home, particularly if the person with Autism turns her aggression on them with any regularity. It can also directly affect the person's health, as finicky eaters, for example, can battle nutrition issues, and others face hygiene issues, if they view bathing routines as "interruptions" in the schedule.

Difficulty in expressing needs; uses gestures or pointing instead of words

Many persons on the Autism Spectrum are verbal, and some develop good language skills. Others use sign language or communicate with drawings and pictures. To whatever extent language is used, communicating need is the issue. It is difficult because sometimes the child does not recognize that there is a need. My daughter can have something stuck in her eye and not recognize that she needs help removing it. Or she may step on a splinter, and until she is limping, not recognize that she requires assistance. It is part of the nature of Autism.

Repeating words or phrases in place of normal, responsive language

Some persons who are verbal have echolalia. Jessica was echolalic for years as she was finding her voice. She would repeat the last thing she heard you say. For example, if I told her to get her coat, she would say "Get your coat, your coat, your coat, coat coat coat coat coat coat coat coat coat …" However, she wouldn't get the coat; she was just talking. Sometimes echolalia is limited to the last words of a sentence, or to a misplaced phrase that the person has inserted. My daughter did this for quite a while. She would begin a phrase with "According to my research …" or some other odd vernacular. It made me smile.

Laughing, crying, showing distress for reasons not apparent to others

The areas of the brain that distinguish one emotion from another seem to be highly affected in individuals on the spectrum. When working with Jessica, and later when studying other children with whom I tested my therapy regimen, it was evident that these children felt all the typical emotions but that they could not identify them and call them forth on command. Research at the Center for the Study of Autism (www.autism.org) would suggest that some individuals on the Autism Spectrum are unable to differentiate between emotions as a result of an underdeveloped amygdala, the emotion center of the brain. With patience and conditioning, many individuals on the Autism Spectrum are able to become comfortable with all the colors of emotion that are used in society.

Prefers to be alone; aloof manner

I can't confirm that these kids prefer to be alone, but I know that they are alone. It is my feeling that the most contemporary dictionary terms used to define the standard characteristics of Autism tend to use verbiage such as "individuals *appear* to prefer being alone ..." for this reason. Once Jessica found her words and was able to use them, she confessed that she was very lonely. She longed for a friend. She talked constantly about how alone she felt in "that dark place" – I refer to it as "The Void." We talk a lot about how frustrating it was for her to not be able to communicate. If you can't communicate, you retreat. This is easily seen by others as aloofness. Perhaps in many cases it is, but in Jessica's case, it was not.

Tantrums

Also called "episodes" or "meltdowns," many times tantrums are outside the control of the person. The tantrums are usually the direct result of a loss of control, due in part to a change in routine. They are often called "storms," because they hit like storms, and sometimes all you can do is dig in and hang on until they pass over. The parents of children with Autism suffer great distress in public by onlookers who fail to understand that the behavior exhibited by their child is not due to their inability to control the child or from a lack of discipline. Many "Spectrum Parents" share stories of being scolded by strangers, or of being reported to local authorities for "bad parenting."

Difficulty in mixing with others

Even the most well-adjusted, highest-functioning individual on the Autism Spectrum has trouble mixing socially. Difficulties involve determining the rules of conversational engagement and reading the signals on the faces of others. Further, humor is often elusive to the Autistic mind, and common word plays don't make sense sometimes. Thus, people on the Spectrum are often the last ones to get the joke if they get it at all. Sometimes, it is difficult to keep in control of the volume level of the voice, so at any time, the person on the Autism Spectrum may inadvertently find himself outside the "proper" social circle, simply because he laughs too loudly, or talks too loudly when nervous.

While it is feasible to learn social skills, it is not a simple matter as there are at least a dozen social rules to remember in any given setting: For example, "don't interrupt when someone else is talking," can be a daunting task for someone on the spectrum. Simple rules of conversation can be confusing for the Autistic mind. Who talks first? When is it my turn? Was that funny? Would it be appropriate to talk about what I heard on the news this morning? Would it be appropriate to talk about my pet? How long do I talk about my pet? What if someone else comes into the conversation? How do I know if the other person is bored? There are so many things to remember! At best individuals on the spectrum usually come across as slightly odd or eccentric. That's fine, because the way I see it, we all are slightly odd in one way or another.

May not want to cuddle or be cuddled

This is one of the most heartbreaking traits that parents of children with Autism have in common, because we love to hug our kids. Many of these kids go rigid if you initiate a hug, others won't let you hug them at all. At the same time, while there are many who resist physical contact of any kind, others on the Autism Spectrum need firm, deep pressure. For these persons, there are many devices with rollers that they can control, or boxes that they can squeeze into. Occasionally, some of them love big bear hugs as they help them to feel calmer.

Little or no eye contact

The majority of children with Autism watch you from the corners of the eye, using their peripheral vision. If you move, they will move to keep you in sight. Some children and adults with Autism may make eye contact from time to time, but have difficulty maintaining eye contact if they are also trying to sustain other sensory stimuli. For example, someone with Autism may need to look away because he needs to concentrate on what has been said and not be distracted by what he is seeing.

Unresponsive to standard teaching methods

Many children with Autism cannot follow a regular teaching regimen. They need additional teaching time. They need a lot of individual attention. They need almost constant re-direction to what they are supposed to be working on, as any slight distraction will throw them out of their learning pattern. However, some can work effectively and benefit from a general classroom setting. Placement decisions should be based on the needs of the individual student, and be included in the child's individualized education program, or IEP. The IEP will include the short-term and long-term education goals agreed upon between the administrators and the parents and teachers, according to federal and state guidelines. The IEP follows the child through high school, and the regular planning meetings should help aid in the transition to adult life.

Sustained odd play

This refers to "play" that nobody really understands except the player. It includes behaviors ranging from turning in circles to lining up crayons end to end on the floor for hours and then putting them away, to stacking blocks without looking at them, or bending a Tupperware lid for three hours. The function of this behavior is that the person on the Autism Spectrum is attempting, in many ways, to "order" things. It helps the child to learn about her environment such as shapes and patterns and to discover the workings of toys. It also establishes a routine that the child can control. It is self-stimulatory in nature, and is play-based. These routines can be readily replaced with educational stimuli.

Spins objects

Anything within reach of the person with Autism will go in circles. The person with Autism is likely to go about in circles, too! The function of this behavior is purely stimulatory, what is known as "stimming." The individual on the Autism Spectrum will "stim" by spinning an object, or by rocking or watching an object that is spinning or that is shiny. The need for stimulatory behavior has been proven for all creatures. It is possible to replace one stimulatory behavior for another, less destructive, less obtrusive, or less socially restrictive one. For example, when she became frustrated, Jessica used to bang her head on the floor or hit herself in the face, which is a self-stimming behavior. She used to rock and flap when she was agitated. She no longer exhibits these behaviors. She has replaced them, and when agitated, now scrunches a pillow with her hands privately in her room, or does deep breathing exercises much like yoga, to relieve stress.

Inappropriate attachments to objects

I mention in Chapter Two (the diagnosis chapter) that Jessica became attached to things at daycare that didn't belong to her, which was some-times inconvenient. This is pretty common among children with Autism. A child may have an affinity for shoes, and insist on sleeping with them (or bathing with them!)

Apparent over-sensitivity or under-sensitivity to pain

Many children with Autism demonstrate hypersensitivity not only to pain, but to every sort of stimulus – sounds, smells – any sort of input coming from the senses. The temperature of the bath water, too hot or too cold by a couple of degrees, does not go unnoticed. The texture of certain foods is often a factor. Children on the Autism Spectrum may gag on sesame seeds if they are on a hamburger bun, or the blackened part of a grilled hot dog if they are accustomed eating them boiled only. They insist that these changes "hurt" them, that they can feel the changes in texture in their mouths. On the other side, many show an under-sensitivity to stimuli, as in the case where a person with Autism gets a splinter in her toe and never mentions it at all, when in fact, it must irritate her greatly.

No real fear of danger

Many persons on the Autism Spectrum are hung up on rules. If they are verbal, they may recite the rules verbatim; however, they often do not realize that the rules apply to them. They do not understand why cars cannot bounce off them as in cartoons, or why they could not walk off the end of the dock onto the surface of the water, when it appears to be as smooth as glass. The nature of their minds is such that people with Autism expect that everyone is able to read what is written inside their mind, also called the "you know what they know" principle. For example, Jessica would expect you to know what she had for breakfast this morning. If a child with Autism were alone in a room and hid a toy inside a box out of your sight, when you entered the room, he might expect you to know that he had hidden the toy and where. Similarly, children are often frustrated when you do not know what they are talking about, because you should already be aware of what they are trying to communicate to you, even if they are not being particularly verbal. To many people unfamiliar with the Autistic Spectrum, this frame of mind seems very foreign. It is almost as if some persons with Autism communicate on a different plane of existence at times.

Given this frame of mind, it shouldn't be surprising that when dangerous situations arise around them, persons on the Autism Spectrum may not be aware of it at all. They simply never know that there is a reason to be afraid. Those of us familiar with the Spectrum are all too accustomed to seeing an individual with Autism wander out into traffic, seemingly oblivious to the cars as they screech to a halt and blow their horns. The individual with Autism cannot process or interpret the looks of bewilderment, shock, or anger on the faces of the drivers. Instead she assumes that the driver knows that it was Monday, and 3:00 p.m., and that it was her turn to cross the street. The driver knew her intention, of course, he just forgot to stop his car. She is "very upset, but will forgive the driver as long as he remembers to stop his car next time. That driver needs to be more careful!" Based on such "reasoning," a person with Autism continues to cross the street against traffic, oblivious to the danger of which she has no real fear.

Noticeable physical over-activity or extreme under-activity

Individuals on the Autism Spectrum sometimes have bursts of energy and bursts of creativity. Many insist on the same routine, and can be seen frantically going through certain parts of their day, and then seeming to drag through other parts. By the same token, those who are higher functioning may have long periods of activity, where they are working diligently on tasks, but lack the organizational skills to see them through to the end. They leave one thing unfinished to move on to the next. They collect jumbled stacks and piles of papers, most of them crumpled. You may observe an individual on the Autism Spectrum running in circles, or back and forth for hours. Suddenly she might laugh out loud for a long time, and then sit and rock, staring into space.

In some cases, the behavior is part of a larger pattern that has yet to be uncovered. A burst of energy by an individual on the Autism Spectrum that occurs every afternoon at about the same time may be part of that person's inherent routine that he has determined for himself. For example, I discovered that Jessica was sitting in the same spot in her room, very still, at about the same time every afternoon. It was a routine that she had established for herself, and I discovered that she was following the afternoon sun on the floor. During this time, she would be otherwise unresponsive to our therapy. Moving "venues," or going to another room, and changing the routine, while it upset her at first, re-established for her that the routine she had set for herself wasn't the one that she needed to follow for the remainder of her life. Rather than sitting in the sunlit spot of her bedroom floor, it was better to learn to adapt to the world so that she could run outdoors every afternoon and enjoy the sunlit backyard.

Uneven gross-/fine-motor skills

Parents of children on the Spectrum often tell stories of how their children are unable to do simple motor activities that other children can do at a particular age, such as stand or hop independently on one leg, use cups and spoons, or dress themselves. However, those same children may be doing unbelievably gifted things like playing music, drawing, building, or lining up toys in a very complicated fashion.

Not responsive to verbal cues; acts as if deaf though hearing tests in normal range

This was the last trait on the ASA list, and when I first read it, a few months before Jessica was diagnosed, I literally burst into tears. After more than two years, dozens of specialists, hundreds of hours of therapy, countless procedures in three states, surgery, and too many dead ends to remember, we were finally on the right track. This had been the first indication that something was wrong. When she was 19 months old, I was afraid that there was something wrong with her hearing.

The list provided by ASA mentioned a "devastating myth" that children with Autism could not show affection. It further stated that children with Autism can and do give affection, but that it requires patience on the part of the parents to accept and give love on the child's terms.

You will read in our story how Jessica and I first reached each other on her terms, and then on mine. She was a child whom I couldn't touch. Tonight, as I write, she sits next to me, her head on my shoulder. We like to cuddle. She loves hugs; she is a great hugger. It took a lot of conditioning. It is perhaps my favorite part of the story. We look at each other now and we smile, remembering.

When I was searching for the answers to Jessica's problems, I found myself trying desperately to find somebody who knew what the trouble was. Nobody really knew how to help us until we got to Division TEACCH. TEACCH stands for the Treatment and Education of Autistic and related Communication handicapped CHildren. At the time that Jessica was diagnosed in North Carolina, the school system was prevented from making final diagnoses for Autism. They referred all the cases to TEACCH, the world standard, and the authority on the subject at that time. Luckily, that program set us out on the right foot.

Until that time, most professionals labeled Jessica with something called "PDD," or Pervasive Developmental Disorder. "PDD" was a label or designation that was a point of great contention among professionals at the time. Since then, any defining diagnosis of PDD, including Autism, has been based upon the *Diagnostic and Statistical Manual of Mental Disorders* (DSM IV-TR, 2000), published by the American

Psychiatric Association in Washington, DC. That's the main diagnostic reference of mental health professionals in the United States.

Five main categories fall under PDD now. It is important to note that PDD is not a diagnosis. It is a "group" with five "subgroups" that come underneath it. That's where Autism falls. The other four are Rett's Disorder, Childhood Disintegrative Disorder, Asperger's Syndrome, and Pervasive Developmental Disorder – Not Otherwise Specified (PDD-NOS).

The symptoms and characteristics for all five disorders overlap in some areas, but are distinct in others, but because they are all pervasive developmental disorders, and thus "related" to one another, treatments are similar.

Families living with Autism tell similar stories. Nearly all their stories start with bewilderment because their child began developing normally, and then demonstrated a delay or a regression around the age of 18 months. This regression is usually in the speech area, or in the child's social interaction with others. Then, almost without exception, when a diagnosis is finally made, there are tears and anger and a lot of grief that for most turns to empowerment out of necessity. In the case of families who have lived with Autism for years, there is a great sense of resolution and often overwhelming fatigue. These families have recognized what is truly important, and have learned to trim out what is not necessary. They have little time to waste.

What has been most important in our success is the way we took on Autism. It wasn't just something that affected my daughter. It was mine. It was ours. Autism sits at the table with you. It becomes a family member. Because it is a lifelong condition, it's something that you adjust to. In many respects, any tough challenge is like this: You must prepare yourself mentally or you've lost from the beginning. You must have a "can do" attitude. From the beginning of our journey with Autism, our goal was to create a life with purpose for Jessica – a life that she could be proud of, and that allowed her to be a contributing member of society. Getting past my own grieving, which was ever-present at first, and moving past my self-pity, to a place where I could join the family of Autism and begin helping others along their journeys, was the only way that any good could come from the experiences that I had been through to that point. So my direction became clear.

The family of Autism is just that – a big family. I was astounded by the way I felt the first time I went to a convention and found myself face to face with a hundred others who'd had the same experience I'd had. I had conversations with strangers about things I thought only I had to go through every day. From my years of working and attending conferences, I had many adult friends who were on the spectrum. As I watched them live their lives, I realized that if I could help Jessica to control her behaviors and maintain her composure, she could have a life with real purpose.

And isn't that what all parents ultimately want for their child?

CHAPTER TWO

The Elusive Diagnosis

"Birth to Shutdown, to the 'Big A Word'"

I wasn't ready for the truth that day 10 years ago. It hit me squarely in the face. Autism. I couldn't even see Jessica as tears clouded my view. I could still hear her babbling away and banging blocks together rapidly on the floor. I was just outside her peripheral range, I knew she couldn't see me, so I put my hands over my face and wept.

I mourned for three full days as all the dreams I had for her future died. The things all moms think about when they get pregnant ... "my daughter will be this or that, ballerina and homecoming queen and valedictorian and on to my alma mater and my sorority, and maybe a degree in business; she will be strong and true and, and, and ..." Actually, by the time Jessica arrived in my arms, I only wanted her to be happy with herself and to have a happy life. I figured that happiness is pretty much contingent upon being able to communicate with the people in our world. By the time of her diagnosis, she was unable to do either of these things.

On that day 10 years ago when we were handed the "terrible" diagnosis, Jessica was 4, and our lives were pretty awful. I was severely depressed because of her condition, but worked as best I could to reach her. She was in her own world, which was some place far away from me.

We had a difficult pregnancy. I was severely dehydrated and required hospitalization on three different occasions prior to her delivery. However, as it was my first child and I was young and strong, my doctor didn't see that anything was amiss, so we just went along as scheduled. Jessica was a wonderful 6 lb., 10 oz. baby. Ten minutes after her birth, the attending physician gave her a perfect 10 on the APGAR rating scale. Everyone has a childbirth story; I won't bore you with mine. Let's just say I would have given her a 10 also. She might even have been an 11. She was a great baby.

Jessica did all the things babies are supposed to do. There were no signs that anything was wrong with her. She turned over on time, ate well, had no problems being touched, and her reflexes were fine. She smiled and laughed just like all other babies, responding to everything normally. She made typical sounds, even saying "mama," "juice," and "chocamee" for chocolate, and was identifying colors and counting by 15 months of age. At 18 months, she could put strings of words together like "Mama-no-go-bye-bye!" if she didn't want me to leave. She was clearly a smart baby, and everyone commented on how bright and alert she was. Then everything stopped dead. That's the only way to say it. It got scary.

Very scary.

Over the course of a two-week time period when Jessica was 19 months old, she stopped talking. I can point the two weeks out on the calendar. The child I had known went away and has never returned, even to this day. Those two weeks were a living hell. My sweet girl changed drastically. She wouldn't eat her favorite foods, sometimes she wouldn't eat at all. She wouldn't let anyone come near her except me. She wouldn't let anyone touch her. When I did touch her, my touch seemed to startle her. She would scream at the top of her lungs as if she had been burned by my touch. She would pull at her clothes constantly, as if she didn't like the way they felt against her skin. She didn't want to be around people with blonde hair. She seemed to lose most of her powers of her well-developed speech, and in place of words used gestures and grunting. Occasionally she would say "Maaaa," but there were no more words in her vocabulary anymore. The most disturbing change was that every time she became the least bit upset, she threw herself on the floor, covered the back of her head with her hands, and screamed "NO!"

At the time I was barely 21 years old, living in a small town in south-central Arkansas. I had no experience in developmental disorders of any type. My first fear was that Jessica had been the victim of some sort of abuse at the hands of the childcare workers or other children at daycare. I launched an investigation not unlike a witch hunt in that small town, which did nothing more than upset a lot of people and leave me without suitable daycare. I still had no answers. She needed to see a doctor.

I wondered if perhaps she was suffering an inner-ear problem. I grew up with a hearing problem for which I was double amplified with hearing aids for years, and it was a condition that I feared she could also suffer. I took her to my family doctor. He would know; I could trust him. From the time I was a youngster myself, he had taken care of every malady in our family; every knick and scrape, torn ligaments and allergy shots, yearly physicals and even my very first pap smear. I was now bringing him another generation to care for.

I put my daughter in his arms and told him something was wrong with my baby. "Very wrong," I said. "She is not the same child she was a week ago. Could it be something with her ears?" Inside I was silently screaming. Please, I prayed, don't let it be her ears. I thought of all the problems I had gone through with my ears. Reading my mind, the doctor raised an eyebrow, shaking his head, but he tested her hearing anyway. It was normal. I don't think I registered any reaction at all and that seemed to baffle him. He patted me on the leg. "Lynley," he said, "you're a first-time mother. There is nothing to be worried about. Bring her back when she's 2 if she doesn't improve and I'll recheck her."

Jessica wouldn't turn 2 for five months. That seemed an eternity to wait when I knew in my heart that there was something terribly wrong with my baby. I couldn't wait. I needed to find answers immediately.

Before we started pinpointing the other behaviors associated with her condition, her diagnosis escaped a great many folks. I was becoming more concerned about her because she was deteriorating, right before my very eyes. She twisted her hands into weird positions and turned her body in circles all the time. She would not respond when her name was called. If you tried to talk to her, she would turn her back in response or run away, or hit her face with her hands. Sometimes I found her in her closet banging her head against the inside of the closet door. It was never a hard banging, just kind of a mild thumping against her forehead.

When I found her like that the first time, she had a faraway gaze in her eyes that I dubbed the "thousand mile stare." No matter what I did, I couldn't get her to snap out of the trance. When I lifted her out of the closet, her body was rigid. She felt like a mannequin in my arms.

I remember one evening when I was attempting to get her ready for dinner and her bath. She was humming to herself and seemed to be in a deep trance. I couldn't get her to eat. I tried to feed her for more than an hour, but she kept refusing. I finally resorted to giving her a sippy cup with some applesauce in it. She slurped some of it and then spit it out. I finally gave up, comforted that I had read that children eventually eat when they are hungry enough.

I then ran a bath for her. The water was barely warm, because she'd been reacting strangely to lukewarm water. She allowed me to undress her rigid body, but when I lowered her into the water, she went berserk. She kicked and bucked, and screeched and clawed at me, and we both went down. She was very strong. There was a sort of wildness in her eyes, an expression of fear in her face. I started talking to her in firm tones, sitting in the water with her, fully clothed. I let her smell the baby shampoo, the baby wash we always used, familiar smells; let her see the toys she always played with. No dice. I eventually pulled the plug, and let the water drain. In the meantime, I continued to hold onto her, wondering what to do. She had to be bathed. With the water gone, she started to calm down a little. I ran the water a little and lathered a washcloth and bathed her while she screamed her head off. I rinsed her with a cup. I bathed her like this for weeks, except I didn't get into the tub after that first night unless it was absolutely necessary. The screaming lessened bit by bit but she didn't like it any better. So, we were in for at least 15 minutes of screaming each night just to take a bath.

But it wasn't just the bath; it was everything else, too. Every seemingly typical activity brought on a screaming fit. By Christmas, just a little over three months from the date of that doctor's visit, she wouldn't talk at all anymore. She'd only point and grunt, and if you took too long to figure out what her grunting meant, you could expect a screaming fit. She woke me up by pulling my hair; she led me around the house, pointing, grunting and shrieking. It took everything short of a fist fight to get her into some clothing besides her nightgown and to get her hair and teeth brushed.

Because I had to work and was trying to go to school part time, Jessica had to go to daycare. I had a hard time finding places for her, because of the constant behavior complaints. When I picked her up in the afternoon and got her in the car seat, inevitably, there would be some problem on the way home. We'd see a dog on the side of the road, and she'd attempt to climb out. I frequently had to stop and crawl in the backseat and restrain her. And forget stopping to run errands anywhere. Once I picked her up, it was home, and no place else. We had a schedule to keep.

I found myself doing anything necessary to avoid the screaming fits. I would stay in whatever room she seemed to need me, and allow her to lead me through the house. I would permit her to grunt and point, and give her the things that she wanted. I could tell what these things were – after a while, a mother just knows what the gruntings mean. It was tedious, and by the end of the day, I was often too tired to fight her any more.

Jessica grew worse. It became increasingly more difficult to take her out in public. Even small things set her off, and I never knew what those things were going to be. It quickly reached the point where I couldn't even take Jessica to visit my parents' house because we were certain to have some sort of ordeal, and it was easier on everyone if we remained at home.

At Easter, my family gathered at a local restaurant after church services. Everybody was dressed up and ready to celebrate; Jessica was all decked out in a cute little dress with a matching basket and all the trimmings. But we never got to eat. Looking back on it, I think now that it might have been that the colors of the room resembled those in a doctor's waiting room, or maybe it was the smell of the cleaning agents used in the restaurant. We will never know for certain, but whatever it was, it caused Jessica to go rigid and begin to shriek. As soon as she was outside the room, she was fine again.

To someone looking on, it might have seemed that I had no control over my child. In that small town many undoubtedly muttered under their breath that a sound spanking would be all that was needed. I stuck my head inside the room, blew kisses to my family, whispered apologies to my grandmother and mother, and took Jessica home to eat hot dogs for lunch on Easter Sunday. It was the last time we tried to eat out for a very long time.

I still had no idea that Jessica had Autism. I didn't even know what Autism was. Well, I had seen the movie *Rain Man*, but I didn't connect Autism as it was portrayed in the movie to my child. I knew that there was something very wrong with Jessica, but I was still the only one who believed that. I never gave up trying to reach her, even though she was slipping further and further away every day.

Slowly, she and I fell into a routine without my really being aware of it. This routine was broken dramatically when we moved the following summer to Tennessee, and she got a new room in a new house. This confused her terribly. She didn't eat for almost a week, and cried herself to sleep every night. I thought it was homesickness, attributed it to normal childhood distress and dismissed it.

She still wasn't talking or making eye contact, and wouldn't allow me to talk with her about the changes. I felt at a loss. I would go into her room and follow her as she walked away from me in circles, talking in her direction, hoping for some sign that she recognized me, some evidence that she acknowledged what I was saying, that she understood me. It was like talking to a fish tank – all I got was that same blank stare the guppy gives you as he swims away from you, following his own reflection in the glass.

I missed Jessica so much. She was physically in the house with me, but I felt as though she was gone. I fed her and bathed her every day, but she was missing. I was miserable. Where was my child?

We were now living in a small town not far from Memphis. I began calling specialists nearby before our boxes were even completely unpacked. The move had done something to Jessica, jostled something, I thought. It was time to get serious. I went to the library and checked out books on childhood behavioral disorders. I took Jessica from one specialist to another. Test after test after test ensued – everything from EEGs to brain stem response testing to eliminate the possibility that she had seizure disorders.

I took her to speech therapists. This turned out to be a waste of time because Jessica wouldn't talk; she wouldn't even look at them. Next, I tried occupational therapy. I was willing to attempt anything to try to reach her, but it seemed futile. Sometimes they would have good luck getting a response from her, at other times, she would refuse to even go into the room. It depended on what kind of day we were having. She also had days that were great: She would laugh and smile, and toss her little head, and the therapists would think she was darling. She still behaved as though they were not in the room, but some days she interacted slightly, which gave us hope.

I continued to read everything I could find on the subject of developmental delay. No one could pin down the problem beyond the general diagnosis of developmental delay-not otherwise specified. Many told me that it was too early to tell what was wrong.

Jessica's emotional storms could come on suddenly. I began to notice that on "borderline" days, strong perfume could trigger emotional outbursts. Sometimes when I was sitting in a doctor's waiting room and someone came in wearing perfume, I had to wave these people away from talking to Jessica in hopes that they wouldn't set her off. I would have loved to have had time to explain in more detail why they couldn't come close and snuggle with my sweet child. Instead, I had to wave them off, saying, "Please stay away from her or she'll have a fit, thanks." At other times, I had to scoop her up and whisk her out the door when a fit came on, with little time to listen to the apologies of the sweet little ladies who were trying to talk to her or pat her little blonde head. Some days she was okay in public, and some days she wasn't. It was very frustrating, Jessica seemed to be as frustrated as I was.

Many times I could tell that she was trying to say something, but couldn't get the message out. I saw such intelligence. I would continue to talk to her, as though she understood me, and I would imagine her response. She began to make garbled noises, but they weren't English. They were gibberish; it was a jargon all her own. I began to have some hope that perhaps she would start to insert some of this gibberish in places where an English response should be in a conversation. At least, I thought, perhaps she knew that it was her turn to say something. This would show some demonstrative language learning.

I kept reading, trying to find something in all those books, but I found nothing. There was nothing out there, and in 1992, the Internet was still a fledgling on the subject. So I suspected we would be trailblazing, even then. It seemed too bizarre that all the doctors we had seen couldn't put a name to what Jessica had, and that none of the clinicians could help us. Jessica was still so far away.

As Jessica was approaching her third birthday, I was focusing on the language aspect of her behavior. There had to be something there, I figured, so I made an appointment with a speech clinic. The speech and language therapists whom we were seeing thought that Jessica was delightful even though she wouldn't say anything to them. Her first appointment went well, so we got off to a good start. She even kept the bow in her hair for a reasonable length of time. She fell asleep in the car seat on the way home – I almost had a day most people could describe as normal, aside from taking a child to a speech therapy appointment and having a couple of screaming fits.

The speech therapist remarked that the noises that Jessica made were language-based, confirming what I felt. Still, the noises didn't seem to be English. The speech therapist explained that the noises Jessica was making might eventually sound a little like the English words she had lost, but that it was possible that she would never communicate effectively verbally. So she advised me to prepare myself for that end also.

There was still no concrete diagnosis for Jessica's condition. This was unfortunate for several reasons, among them insurance. We were on the government's insurance by this time, and they refused to approve speech therapy until they received a proper diagnosis. The clinic could not afford to take charity cases, as the business manager explained. They wrote an excellent referral for continued therapy for me to take to the next clinic because we could not pay, the manager added, and sent us away with a smile.

I sat in the parking lot with my head on the steering wheel and Jessica's thick file in my lap. I counted on my fingers … Fourteen months since she shut down. Tick tick tick. Speech delays mean school delays, I knew. Preschool was around the corner. I was reading at her age. I could recite *The Cat in the Hat*. My daughter's language consisted of gibberish. I needed to focus on that. I needed to get back to work …

The gibberish was mangled and muted, reminiscent of sounds made by the hearing impaired when learning to speak. I collected all Jessica's medical records from every doctor, every single piece of paper, even the well-child checkups, and started looking through them. I made a huge list, including every bump and scrape, again looking for clues. I knew I would eventually find something.

The first thing that jumped out at me was a string of ear infections. I thought perhaps we should look into that again; maybe there had been some permanent damage to the lower Eustachian area of the ear. So I went to the medical library. I found some case studies showing that swelling or damage had trapped fluid in that area, preventing sound from being transmitted properly. My hypothesis was that if this were the case with Jessica, perhaps everything she heard sounded as though she were under water. Since children can generally only repeat what they hear, how could she do anything but regress verbally? It made perfect sense to me, and I threw my energies into proving or disproving this hypothesis.

Next came the hard part. I had to find a doctor who would listen to me long enough to try to help Jessica. I was a 22-year-old mother working her way through college, with an out-of-control, shrieking, wiggling child on one hip and a backpack on my shoulders. My marriage to Jessica's father was crumbling because of factors not related to our daughter's condition, but complicated by it nonetheless. Her father loved her and tried to be there for her, but from the beginning, through the endless studying, the research, the appointments and the therapy, it has been just the two of us – Jessica and me.

Sometimes it's like that with conditions like Autism. There are people who can take it and people who are better at standing back and letting others handle it. So when people ask me where her father was when all this was happening, I am truthful. Jessica and I were on the gridiron. We were on the field, squarely in the game at all times. I was the coach; we had a cheering section, people on the sidelines, and people in the stands. Her father was the band director – his back to us and his mind elsewhere most of the time, glancing in our direction at times to lend support and get attention at the appropriate moment. He had a duty to support us, so he was there, but that was about it. She and I are glad that it was just the two of us. If he had been involved, there likely would not have been this book. The processes I developed for Jessica were born of necessity. I had to learn a lot "on the fly," and I had to train others to help me because I was on my own. Necessity was, in this case as in many others, the mother of invention.

We get dealt a bad hand sometimes. Frankly, Autism plays hell on a marriage. Her father and I lived with a level of stress that "regular" couples cannot fathom. To remain sane, you move on and do what needs to be done. Jessica's biological father has not been in our lives for a number of years, and signed over full custody to me so that my present husband could adopt her. He recognized the need to do what was in her best interest, and did what he could to accomplish that. At the time when she needed diagnosing, we were too young to handle both her needs and each other's needs. I bear him no ill will.

So I hunted for an ear-nose-throat specialist, or "ENT," and I finally found one who decided to give me the benefit of the doubt: Dr. Gayle Woodson at the University of Tennessee Medical Systems, the UT Medical Group, in Memphis. She listened to my hypothesis and looked at my list. I had everything in Jessica's medical file organized in the same order as my list, with highlights and sticky notes to show the pattern I had found. Dr. Woodson noticed something that I didn't know to look for: A staph infection just before the ear infections had become serious. Sometimes these bacteria can set up housekeeping in other places in the body. In Jessica's case, the staph bacteria had manifested in her tonsils. Her tonsils weren't red or sore, but they were gigantic. They were probably trapping fluid in her ears on both sides.

It was decided that what was needed was a tonsillectomy, and probably removal of the adenoids at that time. We scheduled to have this done at LeBonheur Children's Medical Center in Memphis. The surgery went well, although it was a bit of an ordeal. Dr. Woodson and the medical professionals at UT Medical Group were amazing. It is my belief that we were able to eliminate many dead ends very quickly because of Dr. Woodson's quick response to our need. I also have to commend her for recognizing that there was something not working right with Jessica. We were being shuffled about, and medical professionals weren't taking me seriously because of my youth, or because I shouldn't know anything because I wasn't a doctor. Dr. Woodson is a woman of great vision, and was willing to do her job as a physician, and take care of my daughter. We found out that we were scheduled to be moved by the military a short time following Jessica's surgery; as a result, Dr. Woodson would be unable to follow up with her care. Nevertheless, she pushed appointments to the front of the line so that we could be taken care of promptly before we had to leave, and still have adequate time to prepare, and to pack. I have never been so grateful to a physician before or since.

Weeks passed and Jessica began to make improved sounds, so the doctors and I assumed that we had been on the right track in thinking that the problem was eliminated with the removal of the tonsils. She would have clearer sounds to replicate verbally because she could hear better, we thought. In the meantime, I waited and worked diligently with her. But I soon was puzzled that she didn't seem to be making much progress. Her sounds were different, but they weren't any closer to English than before. I continued to work with her on consonant sounds, trying to help her differentiate between them. I also began to work with her with the *Hooked on Phonics* musical tapes, but she showed little interest.

Daycare continued to be a constant struggle. Although the workers would say that she was a good girl, she had problems. She never wanted me to leave, so I had to be very creative with my departures.

For the most part, she did not interact with the other children. When she did, it would consist of taking toys and other objects from the others. She became attached to these objects and failed to give them up again. It was beyond just a failure to share, because giving them up at the end of the day was more than just an average struggle as well. She often wanted to have them with her for days at a time, not wanting to have them out of her hand to eat or bathe. If they fell out of her hand in sleep, it would awaken her! And as suddenly as she became attached, she would become unattached and lose interest. Then the item could be returned. It was particularly frustrating if the item was a piece of clothing, even more so if the item was soiled, and more so if soiled by another child.

Finally, discipline became an issue at daycare because the other children realized that Jessica was an easy mark. She was singled out because she had a funny little giggle and seemed willing to play at first, as long as the other children didn't attempt to touch her, but never understood the rules of the game. Therefore, she was the first to be left out, or became the "monkey in the middle" with the others picking on her. No wonder she soon hated going to daycare. When I picked her up in the evening, it was usually a few minutes of scathing "you left me" betrayal hanging between us along with copious tears. I was also aware that the daycare facility was happy to take my money in exchange for the hours that she was kept there, but there was little exchange. She was merely captive inside a world of her own design.

Soon it was time to move again – this time to North Carolina where her father was newly stationed. We had a new house. Again, she had a new room, and a new daycare setting. The new daycare worker was Miss Kelly, a wonderful woman who was very caring, but who agreed that Jessica was in her own little world.

It wasn't much different once Jessica was picked up in the afternoons from daycare. Other people in Jessica's world flitted in and out, attempting to interact with her, feeding her, talking at her, changing the movie in the VCR, responding to her pointings and gruntings, but otherwise just moving in and out of her world in shadow. She never looked them in the face or called them by name. That included me. I was just another shadow after a while. I think she was more familiar with my smell than anything else. She would react strangely if I used a different perfume or a strong-smelling lotion. She would spin in the kitchen if I burned strong-smelling candles. After a while I wondered if she was looking for me in her peripheral vision because she couldn't smell me over the scent of the candle. There were many odd behaviors like this, none of them leading to definitive answers.

In fact, much of her behavior could be described as odd. She would rock back and forth. She would spin in circles and, if given the chance, would spin objects on the floor or on the table in circles. She banged her head on the floor, the table, the walls, or on your leg if you got close enough. At times she would hit herself in the face with her hands. She flailed and shook and shrieked, laughing in between for no reason. She made no eye contact. She refused human contact, and went rigid if you initiated it. When you had to pick her up, she was hard to hold, and squirmed away from you. We had major difficulty with toilet training because she didn't seem to mind being wet or soiled, and with the complication of communication added to the mix, it was a bad situation.

In retrospect, I can look at these indicators and see that they scream "Autism." But at the time, nobody connected Jessica's behavior to Autism.

It was now time to talk about preschool. We had the summer to work on verbal skills. I continued to work with her on *Hooked on Phonics*. It seemed that we watched *Sesame Street* around the clock, because those videos were in the VCR constantly. To see if she would begin to use more English words, I labeled everything in the house. I refused to respond to her pointing and grunting.

I thought I was reaching the breaking point one day, trying to get her to keep using a sippy cup, when it was evident that what she really wanted was a bottle of juice. She kept pointing and grunting, getting more and more persistent and pushy about it. It was clear that she was approaching a full screaming bout. I picked her up, bringing her face to my level, where she could get the full impact of my words. It was a move I had never made before – I was hoping that it would get her attention. I told her that I would gladly get her a bottle if she would ask for a bottle. She had to say it in English. "I know what you want. I don't care how long you point and grunt and scream. Say bottle and you get a bottle." I said that last part over and over again, maybe 10 times, before I put her down again and walked away. She remained where I had put her down, and then shocked me to the core. In perfect English, it came, "Bottle."

I dropped the laundry basket. I ran to the cabinet and produced a bottle and filled it with juice. Never mind that she was 3 years old. The child asked for a bottle! I plopped down right there, cross-legged on the kitchen floor, and wept and prayed my prayers of thanksgiving. I knew that something had just happened that was significant. I hadn't heard a clear English word in almost two years. I count this word as the second word that she spoke, with "Mama" being her first at the age of 7 months.

A few weeks passed before I had to register her for preschool. It was at this time that we met one of the most intuitive and influential people who would ever come into our lives. Her name was Lisa Craver. She sat on the committee who looked over Jessica's file the day that we went into the Cumberland County Schools with our label of pervasive developmental disorder – not otherwise specified. The others floated in and out of our lives, as many in various school settings do. There were two administrators from the Cumberland County Schools present besides Lisa Craver, and they sat on one side of the long table intended for children. I sat on the other side. We all sat half-crouching in miniature chairs.

Jessica played with the many toys in the room. At the beginning of the meeting, Lisa spent some time talking with Jessica and watching her play. It was a good day for Jessica: she was in a good humor, and she had spoken a few words. I had been particularly encouraged lately because she had been identifying colors by pointing to them if you asked which was red or which was blue. I was certain that all the troubles would soon be just a bad memory. I saw this meeting as a formality; nothing more. Jessica was on her way towards a normal school life.

But it was not to be that way. I sat there smiling in front of Lisa Craver, who showed such compassion on her face as we reviewed Jessica's test scores. Her score on the Stanford-Binet, an IQ test for children, was a 50. They had her labeled now along with the other children who were mentally retarded. It was absurd. I knew that she was not retarded.

I protested. "How can a verbally based test be used to score a nonverbal child?" All smiles were now gone. It may never have occurred to anyone present that a parent could be well versed in the testing mechanisms themselves. Lisa Craver was the only one to break the uncomfortable silence. She asked me if Jessica had been tested for Autism. I was shocked to my core. I had never thought a moment about Autism.

"What, like *Rain Man*?" I asked her, incredulous. There was no way. I laughed out loud. I shook my head. But Lisa Craver didn't move; she never changed her expression. It dawned on me that she wasn't kidding.

"Are you serious?" I finally asked, my voice almost a whisper. Again, she didn't change her expression. She said that there was no way to be sure without testing, but that many of Jessica's behaviors were indicative of Autism.

Lisa said, "You may want to get in touch with TEACCH at the

University of North Carolina, especially as we are so close to them. They will have a lot of great information. They are the authority on Autism and communicative disorders. Even if she does not have Autism, they are a good resource, and she should probably be tested anyway." She smiled at me sympathetically.

Despite shock and disbelief, I knew that it was good advice. Nevertheless, I felt angry and confused. Everything seemed upside-down. My ears were ringing. It took a lot of energy to calm myself down and focus on the remainder of the meeting. It seemed that professionals were always trying to tell me one thing after another. They had run test after test, and they'd done years of therapy. They accepted what little money I had, only to give no solution, or to suggest one malady and then another. We'd reached a hundred dead ends. Now some new professionals were suggesting mental retardation and Autism. It was too much to think about. And here was still more stuff to know about, some place called TEACCH.

I went home in a daze. Jessica giggled her disjointed giggle beside me, while jutting her chin out towards the windshield, her hand twisting oddly beside her. She babbled away in her jargon, having a conversation with an imaginary friend, I guessed. I refrained from joining in this time. Instead, I cried silently all the way home. I had to find out more about TEACCH. I had to call them right away. Luckily, Lisa Craver had given me a list of numbers.

I might not have known what TEACCH was that morning, but Lisa educated me. I learned, and in the days and weeks that followed, read everything that I could find on Autism. I soon realized, long before Jessica's diagnosis, that so much of what we experienced was a textbook example of the condition in one way or another. My mother and I shared information and a small library between us, and as painful as it was to admit, it all began to make sense.

TEACCH is a program that started in North Carolina and is run through the University of North Carolina health systems. People come from all over the world for the diagnosis of their children and the education of their families. Diagnostics are very comprehensive. At the time, a team of clinicians was working with just one child per day. The waiting list was more than a year long. They gave us an appointment in Wilmington 15 months in the future.

In the meantime, Jessica received occupational therapy and speech therapy at her new daycare on post at Ft. Bragg. This would continue after school started, but the clinicians would visit her at school instead. She started school at Brentwood Elementary School, as part of the preschool handicap program. Even though she continued to make progress, I decided not to wait. I called and inquired about cancellations at a regular basis, and was able to shorten our waiting time dramatically. We were finally seen at the Wilmington TEACCH Center for diagnosis.

They spent all day with Jessica. The prognosis after testing was guarded. The therapists and the director of the center explained everything, and were as supportive as possible. All the things that I had been reading over the last months came back to me in a flood of ideas; I tried to ask about as many of these things as I could. Would she ever be able to effectively communicate in English? Would we be expected to put her in a self-contained special education class? Would the public schools require her to wear a helmet if she continued to bang her head? Would she be able to earn a high school diploma or the equivalency of a high school education by the age of 21? Would college be possible? Would she require ongoing supervision as an adult, or would we have to consider the possibility of a supported living situation, such as a group home? Or might we be one of those families who would choose to have our daughter remain at home for the rest of our lives?

Jessica's skills were two years behind at least. We had no way to know if she would ever progress beyond the mental capacity of her present level. There were no good answers to all my questions. It was the first time that I would become familiar with the following phrase: "It is impossible to predict the future of a child with Autism." This is a true statement for all children with Autism, and it can inspire great hope if you will allow it. However, and unfortunately for the director, I was asking apocalyptic questions, and wasn't ready for that phrase yet.

Very little of what Jessica was doing was communicative, and no one could know if she would ever communicate effectively in English. Two previous speech therapists had said that she would not. Her current therapists attested to the fact that all she had was echolalia and gibberish, which was not meaningful language. Her communication was nonverbal. Would this change? We did not know, but we would continue to work.

"Okay," I asked. "Could she be high-functioning Autistic, or HFA? I have heard a lot about HFA kids, and I think Jessica might be very bright. You should see what she does with blocks …"

The director smiled patiently. She explained that the term "HFA" was overused. She said that Jessica's skills fell more in the normal range, so she would not be considered high functioning, but that I need not worry about it. She was trying to make me feel more secure perhaps, considering Jessica's Stanford-Binet IQ score of 50. I had asked her if my mentally retarded daughter was high functioning. In my opinion, it didn't seem a strange question. I knew a girl with MR in school who was brilliant.

I remember that exact moment well. The words of Jessica's diagnosis have just landed on me, heavy like bricks and stones; I am devastated. There is a long moment of silence. I hear the sound of the clock ticking on the wall, and the cars are passing on the street outside. I wonder if any of those cars are going to the beach. I wish for an instant that I were going to the beach. I want to be anywhere but where I am, sitting there with my heart breaking.

The director smiles at me kindly. "Do you have any other questions?"

Do I have any other questions? Yes. I have a million questions, but I can't find my voice. There is such a lump in my throat that I can barely breathe, let alone talk. I can't even meet the director's kind gaze. If I do, I'm afraid that I won't be able to get past what she's told me. Yet it's only confirmation of what I had read. But you're not ready for the truth. Of the million questions, all that comes out is "What now?" as she begins to lay out what Lisa Craver and I had already discussed about occupational therapy and speech therapy. We talk about how important it is for the parents to be involved with therapy, to be interested in investigating new treatments, and to take part in support groups.

The director's eyes and mine meet. Then we talk about how much therapy will take place in the schools, and what is available in the community. Her eyes are insistent, silently pleading with me. They tell me that I will be the primary therapist all of Jessica's life. I know this already, but here is my confirmation. I feel a switch inside me turn on. "Every day, all the time! Never let up – Never give up!!" I look again at the list she has given me. I will read every book on that list. I write down phrases she says to me. I will put them on sticky notes. They are my new inspirational phrases. They will keep me going in the weeks to come.

On the ride home, I was still reeling from the blow, but I knew that I couldn't afford to wallow in misery. I had work to do. I could not accept this verdict for Jessica or for myself. I vowed that Autism would not be our life sentence.

My journal entry that night reads as follows:

8/3 TEACCH Diagnostic in Wilmington. Autism. Not HFA (high-functioning Autism); she's in average range. Hard to tell about future. It could go many ways. Talked about possibilities vs. probabilities. There's always hope. Have to cling to hope. Possibilities of – probably not at her current level right now. Possibilities of communication? The director was careful to say she just didn't know. I told her about ST (speech therapist) who said she'd not speak, and she said it was impossible to predict but all agreed that very little of what Jessica does right now is very communicative. Certainly not giving up is key. Kids can turn around with therapy. We talked helmets. Basically it's up to us unless the school mandates it. Behavior? We do what we can. Read ... read ... read. ASNC has a library. There's a will, there's a way. Just gotta be a way. The reality today is that she will maybe get a high school education by age 21, and live with me for the rest of her natural life or mine, then go to a group home or institution. Your basic living nightmare. Wake me up. Show me the hope.

I closed my journal, tucking the book list from TEACCH inside, and left the kitchen table. I pulled the covers over Jessica, who had her Minnie doll hugged firmly to her chest. I picked Mickey off the floor and took him with me to my room, where I crawled into bed myself. I pulled up the covers, hugged Mickey to my chest, said my prayers, and cried myself to sleep.

The next morning, it was time to get moving. I joined the Autism Society of America and the Autism Society of North Carolina. Soon I started attending a local support group for parents of children with Autism and developmental disorders. I was immediately struck by the diversity of the group: rich and poor, young and old, every possible background, the apathetic and the intellectual. Through those doors we all come, and then we are all on equal ground. We all share Autism. We all have it in common. We all have that puzzle to solve. It's watching this that makes me realize that it isn't just our kids who have Autism. Families have Autism. We're all in this together.

Jessica Speaks: On Why I Was Banging My Head

There is no way to explain this so anybody could really understand. Most of the time, the reason I was banging my head was because of noises that I wanted to go away. I am talking about noises like the toilet flushing, or the air coming through the vent in my room. These noises would not allow me to sleep. They would not allow me to think clearly. All I wanted to do was get them out of my head, and the only way I could do that was to bang them out so that I didn't have to concentrate on the noise.

When my mom made it against the rules to bang my head, I would hum instead. I would go into my own little dreamland and think to myself. Sometimes this would let me go to sleep. This was a success, and I am glad that I don't bang my head on things. It hurt. You wouldn't believe the bruises I gave myself. Once I banged my head on a coffee table and made a bruise in the middle of my forehead. That was not pleasant. You can see why I am glad now. Glad is an understatement.

Sometimes I still hear minor noises that distract me. Like most people, I ignore them. It's the right thing to do, and there's a lot less bruising.

CHAPTER THREE

A Little About Chaos Theory

"Because out of Chaos Comes Order!!"

Many people who hear me talk about using chaos theory in my work ask me what it is. It surprises me how few people are aware of what it is. I won't go into any complicated mathematics. The principles of chaos are fairly easy to explain and understand. Chaos is everywhere. It's the "butterfly effect" you may have heard about: A butterfly flapping its wings in Brazil can, through a series of causes and effects, be the start of a storm front in the Gulf of Mexico.

In the early 1960s, meteorologist Edward Lorenz, thought of by most to be the father of modern chaos theory, ran experiments to model the weather. In the process, he wrote simple problems and had a computer solve them. The models were based on actual storms in weather patterns. One afternoon, Lorenz attempted to continue a problem from the day before. He restarted the computer and put in the numbers from the equation again, this time halfway in the middle of the first run. It began just the way it had the day before, but then it diverged wildly!

Nothing else had changed. The problems were the same. All the numbers were the same. The computer was the same. His math was done correctly. It was the very same equation. But very small changes yielded very different results.

It wasn't long before Lorenz began changing very small things in his problems and was able to show how different the outcomes of those small changes could be. Soon, the whole world was talking about Lorenz's butterfly effect.

It's easy to understand how the theory was born in the mind of a meteorologist. The fundamental principle of chaos theory is that although dynamical systems may never repeat themselves, there are patterns nonetheless. That's why no two sugar crystals are alike, and all our thumbprints are different. The patterns are there, we can recognize what we see as a crystal or a thumbprint, but the patterns are not repeating. Each is unique.

It also is an indicator that larger patterns exist all around us that we may or may not recognize as patterns. We have speech patterns, sleep patterns, behavioral patterns, and even patterns in our diet. Each pattern is unique. There are many things that we can be taught to do, and although we may perform a task well, we will never perform it exactly the same way twice. One professional ballet dancer might be asked to do the same round sweeping leap, or tour je'tee 20 times. She would do it differently each time. The arch of her sweeping leg, the placement of the landing foot, the tilt of the chin, even the very speed at which she was moving, would all be slightly different. Yet, to us in the front row of the auditorium, the movements appear flawlessly identical to one another. There is chaos!

In the example of the ballet dancer, if you were sitting in the audience, and knew that the dancer was about to perform the same leap as before, you would be able to predict what it might look like, before she starts. Your mind's eye has seen the previous leap and recorded what it looked like. The next leap looks familiar. You can predict that she will land in approximately the same spot.

But what would happen if a sandbag fell, and startled her in the middle of her preparation for the following leap? What if suddenly the lights went out on the stage? What if someone ran onto the stage and pushed her out of position? These are three examples of how the outcome of her leap would be dramatically altered. It would be safe, then, to assume that if nothing were to disrupt the dancer's attention, all her 20 leaps would look similar to one another. If she were terribly distracted, however, you could anticipate the leaps might appear much different from one another.

I ask these questions in this way to make a distinction between the words "predict" and "anticipate." Meteorologists study the paths of storms. Living in North Carolina taught me a great deal about storms. Every season, we watched the storms carefully, because hurricane season is almost certain to bring great drama to our daily lives. No two hurricanes are the same, yet the National Weather Service can still track, and may predict, which way each storm will travel. When a storm begins, it is often difficult to tell where it will hit on the coast, but it's coming. That much can be seen.

If all the conditions are present for a hurricane, it is safe to say that a storm is coming. How that storm will behave once it is in full swing is a much different matter. That's where I use the word "anticipation." On the news, the weatherperson says that the storm is off the coast and should be arriving some time in the next 24 hours. What exact time? Nobody knows. But the conditions are right, and the storm is in full swing. It is going to hit you. You are anticipating the arrival of the storm.

Hurricanes and storms are very close to what we deal with when we handle an Autistic episode. Until you are skilled at reading the signs, much like predicting the weather, an emotional "storm" or "episode" may seem to come out of nowhere. I imagine this is very much like what people on the coast experienced before accurate predicting of the weather was possible. It would begin to rain rather innocently, and then suddenly all hell would break loose, horses would fly, and homes would float down Main Street.

With Autism, you eventually begin to recognize what conditions have to be present for an emotional storm to occur. When Jessica had her storms, they were loud, long, and violent. I would never leave her. I would find some place to sit or stand near her to wait out the storm. I would picture a lighthouse in my mind, with the beacon turning around and around, and rays of light pouring through the lens on top. I would sit quietly and meditate on that image, sometimes counting the rotations that the light made to keep myself calm. I would tell myself that eventually there would be a moment when I could throw her a rope and reel her back in. To this day, the lighthouse remains a symbol that is present in my home. It is an ever-present reminder that storms may come with vengeance, but the light shines on.

I won't advance into the more complex areas of chaos, but it is necessary to return and touch on one of the basic principles that describe chaos theory. This old saying has been understood for centuries.

> "For want of a nail, the shoe was lost;
> For want of a shoe, the horse was lost;
> For want of a horse, the rider was lost;
> For want of a rider, a message was lost;
> For want of a message the battle was lost;
> For want of a battle, the kingdom was lost;
>
> All for the want of a nail!"

> – Anonymous

So we see in the example that one small detail, a nail, was the thing that lost the entire kingdom; all for the want of a nail. By that same reason, we can think that by changing that one small event (replacing the lost nail), we may be able to achieve a drastically different outcome, and perhaps keep the kingdom intact after all.

If you understand that: (1) patterns exist everywhere in nature and never repeat, and you understand that (2) anticipating behavior is different from predicting it, and finally, if you understand that (3) by changing one thing you can alter several other things, you've got it: You understand chaos.

Chaos theory is quantitative and exponential, like the mind of the Autistic. It is concrete and abstract at the same time. It is important to mathematicians and physicists, computer scientists and statisticians, and is an amazing art form.

We've made it all the way back to Edward Lorenz, the meteorologist. Lorenz studied the chaotic behavior of gases and other viscous matter in the 1960s, and developed a three-dimensional equation now known as the Lorenz Attractor, which is not unlike the weaving motion between the wings of a butterfly. This motion in nature is seemingly random, yet it exists nearly everywhere you look.

This was of particular importance because Lorenz proved that these dynamical, chaotic systems show patterns. They did not repeat, but there were distinct patterns nonetheless. Thus, not only our weather, but also our daily lives and our schedules, can all be affected, and predicted, by studying those things that come before.

Lorenz was not satisfied with the results of the initial experiment, and to test his theory further built a waterwheel, with eight buckets spaced evenly around the rim. There was a small hole in the bottom of each bucket, which were mounted so that they would always face upwards, like the seat of a Ferris-wheel. The entire system was then placed under a waterspout. A stream of water came from the waterspout, and the waterwheel started to spin. Lorenz increased the flow of water, and, as he predicted with his Lorenz Attractor, the increased velocity of the water resulted in a chaotic motion for the waterwheel. It would spin in one direction as before, but then it would jerk about and spin in the opposite direction. The buckets did not fill at the same times; the system was chaotic. A graph of this waterwheel would resemble the Lorenz Attractor.

Lorenz continued to work with his waterwheel, adjusting the flow of the water and achieving different outcomes. What this all said to Lorenz was that once a pattern is identified, if you initiate a different cause (change the stream), you get a different effect (a differing pattern). What this all said to me was that if I could identify the pattern within Jessica's emotional storms, I might be able to change something that could alter the pattern. If I could alter the pattern, perhaps it could be controlled.

Out of chaos, order. What a wonderful concept. As mentioned in Chapter Two, when seeking a diagnosis for Jessica, I got persistent about writing everything down. It became a habit with me … about everything. I recorded everything that related to Jessica, and after we had her diagnosis, I followed her around with a notebook, writing down everything – from the weather, to what she ate and what time she ate, to the poly/cotton content of her clothing and what colors she was wearing. I recorded the fits she had, and marked their severity. I marked her sleeping patterns. I wrote down who was in the room with her, where they were sitting, and what kind of cologne they were wearing. In addition, I had her teachers and therapists write a daily summary to keep us all in direct contact. That let the teachers know what I was doing at home, and kept us all working toward the same goal. It was tedious and almost drove everyone around us crazy.

Example of Daily Observation Sheet for Jessica

Time	Activity	Place	Food	Other
6:00 a.m.				Cool – 56 degrees
6:15 a.m.	Gets up 620			Potty
6:30 a.m.	Breakfast	Kitchen	Oatmeal, milk	
6:45 a.m.	70/30 poly/cotton			Red shirt & jeans
7:00 a.m.	Singalong video	room	ice box	Socks and shoes
7:15 a.m.	Brush teeth			Screaming
7:30 a.m.	Driving			Some words
7:45 a.m.	Drop off	school		"kitty" "van"
8:00 a.m.				
8:15 a.m.				
8:30 a.m.	Speech therapy	w/Lisa Craver		Great work
8:45 a.m.				
9:00 a.m.	Snack time		Baby carrots	Eats them all – 5/6
9:15 a.m.	Bathroom break			Loud screaming
9:30 a.m.				
9:45 a.m.				
10:00 a.m.				
10:15 a.m.				
10:30 a.m.				
10:45 a.m.				

Time	Activity	Place	Food	Other
11:00 a.m.	Lunch	School	Chick nuggets/fries	Eats ketchup w/spoon
11:15 a.m.	Naptime			Hums–no sleep
11:30 a.m.				
11:45 a.m.				
12:00 p.m.	Video time		Fruit juice pops	Glued to TV set
12:15 p.m.				
12:30 p.m.				
12:45 p.m.	Incident	Another child bumps into her		Storm (episode)
1:00 p.m.	Taken from room	To kitchen	Given carrots & juice	Mom called
1:15 p.m.	Early pickup	To college w/me		Chattering–red face
1:30 p.m.	Driving			Falls asleep in van
1:45 p.m.	Waiting for class	Music practice rm./We play piano		I explain rules in class
2:00 p.m.	Methodist College Chorus	Choir room	Peanut butter crackers	
2:15 p.m.				
2:30 p.m.				Potty
2:45 p.m.				
3:00 p.m.				
3:15 p.m.				
3:30 p.m.	Smiles at Mr. Porter!		Grape Sucker fm Travis	She likes coming here!
3:45 p.m.				Counts steps leaving
4:00 p.m.	Driving home			Falls asleep in van
4:15 p.m.	Arriving home			Agitated–runs in
4:30 p.m.	Sitting in room	bedroom floor		Staring into space
4:45 p.m.	Therapy	Living room		Hooked on Phonics

Time	Activity	Place	Food	Other
5:00 p.m.	Therapy	Living room		Hooked on Phonics
5:15 p.m.	Therapy	Mom's room		"Look at Me"
5:30 p.m.	Video	Her bedroom		Lion King
5:45 p.m.				
6:00 p.m.				Potty
6:15 p.m.				
6:30 p.m.	Dinner	Kitchen	Pot roast & potatoes	Ate three full plates
6:45 p.m.				
7:00 p.m.				
7:15 p.m.	Bath time			Potty, then crying ...
7:30 p.m.	Washing hair			Screeches
7:45 p.m.	Therapy	Her bedroom	Juice box	Barbie interaction
8:00 p.m.	Playing	Her bedroom		
8:15 p.m.				
8:30 p.m.	Brushing teeth	Bathroom		Bites Mom
8:45 p.m.				
9:00 p.m.	Sing songs	Her bedroom		Listens quietly
9:15 p.m.				Asleep by 9:10
9:30 p.m.	Bedtime			

I used a daily sheet that looked something like the previous chart. At the beginning I was using a planner with ready-made sheets that went from 8:00 a.m. through 8:00 p.m. I used the top margins and the "notes" section at the bottom of the page to make them look something like the chart. The above information has been transferred from my planner. The original was in my "shorthand." There are days in this planner that appear to be more behaviorally challenging, and there are days when it is evident that I was studying for a test, or may have been dealing with a substitute teacher because I don't have the school report written down. Parents have days like that. The day represented above is "right in the middle and selected fairly randomly." It was a Monday.

To trace a pattern I used a matrix. Since I have begun to assist other parents in using this system, I have discovered that the quickest way to trace the pattern is to use a transparency sheet like the ones you use for overhead projector presentations. Use a marker to indicate the pattern for one day, and simply lay it over the next day. Transparencies are convenient, because a behavior pattern will become evident over time.

For things that happen frequently throughout the day, such as meals and therapy-type sessions, you need different ways to gauge progress than for things like the weather. However, it is sometimes helpful to have them on the same page. I can often tell if Jessica is going to be moving slowly because she would rather stay indoors with the air-conditioning when it is very hot outside. Similarly, before he overcame his fear of the sky, and of rain, my son Averie did not perform well when it was cloudy. He was afraid that it would start raining later in the day, and was unable to focus on anything else. Cloudy days were worse than rainy days. Often, when I look back at these old behavioral charts, I am glad that I included weather indicators because they speak volumes about what my children were thinking, but might not be saying out loud.

The larger matrix that I used looked a bit more complex. I had to assign a number to every item on the smaller time matrices. Then, several days can be seen throughout the week, or throughout the month.

You may come up with a numbering system that works better for you. If you find something you can remember; use it. I decided that since there were 52 weeks in each year, the first number of the indicator would be whatever number week we were in. The week number was printed on my planner already, so I didn't have to figure that number out. The next character in the indicator told me the day of the week. I was only using one character to do this. I decided to use the following:

M – Monday
T – Tuesday
W – Wednesday
R – Thursday
F – Friday
S – Saturday
U – Sunday

From there, it wasn't difficult. I was already writing down everything Jessica was doing … all the input and output. It wasn't long before I had large matrices for various areas of Jessica's daily life that looked somewhat like this.

Sample Extended Matrix for Jessica

Time	Sleeping in Van	Biting	Staring into Space	Storms (full-blown episodes)
6:00 a.m.				
6:15 a.m.				
6:30 a.m.				
6:45 a.m.				
7:00 a.m.		13M 14U		
7:15 a.m.		14S 15R		
7:30 a.m.	13M 15F	13S 15M		
7:45 a.m.	14M 14W 15R			
8:00 a.m.	13F			
8:15 a.m.				
8:30 a.m.				
8:45 a.m.				
9:00 a.m.				13M
9:15 a.m.				13S
9:30 a.m.				
9:45 a.m.				
10:00 a.m.				13F
10:15 a.m.				
10:30 a.m.				
10:45 a.m.				14W

Time	Sleeping in Van	Biting	Staring into Space	Storms (full-blown episodes)
11:00 a.m.				15S
11:15 a.m.				
11:30 a.m.				14U
11:45 a.m.				15F
12:00 p.m.				13M
12:15 p.m.				
12:30 p.m.				15U
12:45 p.m.				15M
1:00 p.m.				
1:15 p.m.				15T
1:30 p.m.	15M			
1:45 p.m.				
2:00 p.m.				14S
2:15 p.m.				
2:30 p.m.				
2:45 p.m.				
3:00 p.m.				
3:15 p.m.				
3:30 p.m.			14U 15U	14M 14R
3:45 p.m.			13S 13U 14S 13T	15T
4:00 p.m.	13T 13R 14T 15M		13M 13W 13R 13F 14M 14T 14F 13W	
4:15 p.m.	15F		13T1 3F 15W 15S	13T 13U
4:30 p.m.			15M 14R	13W 14F
4:45 p.m.				14R 15W

Time	Sleeping in Van	Biting	Staring into Space	Storms (full-blown episodes)
5:00 p.m.				14S
5:15 p.m.				14W
5:30 p.m.				
5:45 p.m.				
6:00 p.m.				
6:15 p.m.				13R
6:30 p.m.				
6:45 p.m.				14F
7:00 p.m.				
7:15 p.m.				
7:30 p.m.				15R
7:45 p.m.				14T
8:00 p.m.				
8:15 p.m.		13F 13U		
8:30 p.m.		15M 15R 14S		
8:45 p.m.		14F		
9:00 p.m.				
9:15 p.m.				
9:30 p.m.				
9:45 p.m.				
10:00 p.m.				
10:15 p.m.				
10:30 p.m.				
10:45 p.m.				

These are just a few examples of how you can take a few pages from your life and see the behavioral pattern emerge that you may not have been aware of. When you see the pattern, you realize how significant 15 minutes can be to a child who has established a routine for herself, like Jessica did. She had become used to sitting in her room and staring into space at about the same time every day. While it can be argued in many cases that time alone is a creative outlet for some children, the time that Jessica spent in her room sent her into a kind of regression every afternoon. She became withdrawn and was resistant to shifting into new tasks. It was following her and establishing her patterns that alerted me to this part of her routine and how it affected her. Watching the pattern emerge on paper was astounding.

Once everything had received a numerical qualifier and was placed on a matrix. I looked for patterns. I found some food combinations that I thought might be contributing to her hyperactivity. I also saw, right in front of my eyes, the way that her routine had progressed and solidified. It was like watching her place the cinderblocks around us, one by one.

So now, what to do with it? Remember chaos theory? Find the pattern and then manipulate and control it. You've all manipulated patterns yourself at home by grabbing the end of your bed sheet and flipping it upward, then watching it drift back down over your body. Have you ever gotten the sheet to come back down perfectly even on either side of your body? Chances are slim. And there was always that one wrinkle or two in the middle. Before you fluffed the sheet, it was in disarray; there were patterns, although you didn't recognize them as patterns. There was a pattern in the weave of the sheet, in your breathing, in the time lapse since you last slept, in the color combination between the hues in the room, perhaps in the music in the background, and maybe even symmetry in the layout of the room. (There was also a time lapse since you last fluffed the sheet. Think about that one.) We all have behavior patterns like this. People who know me well can attest that I think that everyone is Autistic in some way.

Manipulate and control it … I had to decide whether or not to seek the screaming fit instead of seeking to avoid it. I would later call this technique "hunting the monster." If I could manipulate the fit, perhaps I could help her to control it. What did I have to lose in trying? Nothing, really; it would either work or it wouldn't. All I would lose is whatever peace we had between us, which wasn't much to begin with. On the other hand, what was there to be had, if we succeeded? What did she stand to gain, with even the smallest success? Everything! It was worth it.

From the beginning, I used manipulatives, small toys or other objects, for Jessica to hold or turn in her hands to prevent her hands from flapping. Many times, she immediately dropped these objects. It was when I began experimenting with differing colors and textures that I hit upon something that would point to a major peak in our pattern. One of the objects that I tried was a cat toy, a rubber ball with a bell inside which was bright red in color. She looked directly at that ball for three to four seconds longer than at any other toy or manipulative. I also noticed that she responded to other toys that were red, and to dolls that wore red clothing.

Early in our sessions, a member of our team, Candice, had repeatedly failed to interact with Jessica during their time together. After two weeks of trying everything she knew to do, Candice told me, with tears flowing, that she would not return and waste any more of my time. I believed that this young lady would be a good part of the team, and was worried about where to find a fill-in for her time slot. Racking my brain, and grasping at straws, I asked her to try something. I went to my bedroom to find a red tee-shirt. I asked if she would mind wearing the shirt and spending another five minutes with Jessica to say goodbye. Candice agreed, and for the very first time Jessica looked at her that afternoon. Candice decided to stay on the team, and to regularly wear a red blouse!

Ironically, if Candice had quit working with Jessica then, it would have been several more months before Jessica would read. Candice was the only other member of the team besides me who was working with the *Hooked on Phonics* method with Jessica. She was an important part of Jessica's success.

To help with Jessica's regimen, I had recruited help from friends at the college I attended. Several were from the special education department; others were working on various psychology projects. I let them use the hours of therapy with Jessica as the practicum that they needed, and they often offered their services for free. That was a good thing, because I was broke. Besides, because they were students, they followed my instructions to the letter. That, too, was a good thing.

Jessica was surrounded by people who cared about her, and cared about her progress. She had a lot of friends. These were people who knew and loved her, and who knew and loved me. They watched us struggle and work, and consequently got on board and worked with us as much as they could. Everyone worked as a team, for Jessica's best interest. Everyone celebrated her successes with her. She soon was like a little sister to everyone on the team.

In the first few months following Jessica's diagnosis, as I was learning about Autism, our routine was the immovable constant. I am immediately reminded of Dustin Hoffman in *Rain Man*, and his rocking, mumbling "gotta watch Wapner …" That's what went through my head when Jessica got that look in her eye. She knew when it was time to go home, time to eat, time to bathe, time for bed, time to go to Kelly's, time to leave, time to have a snack. She would look for me in the kitchen at the appropriate times. If we weren't getting ready to leave at the right time, it wasn't good. We couldn't leave early. We couldn't leave late. If the phone rang as we were leaving, I couldn't answer it. Too bad; it was time to leave.

When I made the decision to initiate chaos, I would be grabbing the bed sheet and fluffing all the wrinkles out. I would be stirring things up. No more routine. We wouldn't do things in order any more. I wrote down what time we did things, and then made certain to do them in a different order the following day, and at a different time of day by at least 15-20 minutes. I refused to be led around by points and grunts. Every time I would tell her that I loved her, but I would say "not right now." I had to be the controller.

Yes, it was hard. In fact, it was excruciatingly had. For a while, I wondered if I was doing the right thing, but Jessica slowly began to make some progress. She did just as I expected. She bucked without the routine, and was livid that she didn't receive immediate gratification. When it was normally time to eat, she would be waiting in the kitchen. I would look at the matrix and decide that tonight we would take a bath before dinner. Except tonight, maybe we wouldn't wash her hair. Every day was different from the previous one. She never knew what to expect.

For someone on the Autism Spectrum, this can be extremely confusing. They create this environment around them and, in many ways, we as caretakers enable them to remain in the environment they create, which leaves them unprepared for the world in which the rest of us live. I am not attacking parents and caretakers; I am one myself. I am merely trying to explain my motivation for shaking up Jessica's world the way I did. She was upset … a lot of the time. And I was upset … a lot of the time. But I was convinced that if I could manipulate the pattern, I could control the behavior. I am happy to say that it worked.

I call this process "hunting the monster" because it was going in search of the screaming fit, for the most part. The first few nights were the worst. Jessica's routine had been disrupted, and she started screaming at the top of her lungs. I told her that I would be standing my ground, that I was on her team, but that I was prepared to be up all night long with her if that was what would be necessary. If she was going to scream all night, I would be right there with her. The first night, she screamed until 5:30 a.m. I sat there all night with her, unmoving, and unwavering – like a lighthouse in a raging storm. She finally wore herself out and went to sleep. I scooped her up and put her to bed. Then I collapsed into bed myself.

The next day was tough because she was tired, and our routine was already off kilter because of the time spent making up for lost sleep. When she started screaming, I sat down and prepared to wait it out. It didn't take too long before she realized that it would only be tiring for her. She wasn't going to wear me down. Soon, she allowed me to pick up where I'd left off and continue with whatever therapy I had planned. After a month's time, Jessica had grown tired of all the screaming as part of the routine. Or maybe her throat hurt her. Whatever the reason, she no longer bucked me when I suggested what we would do and when we would do it.

She slowly became accustomed to chaos. Once she was no longer embedded in the routine, the fits slowly become more subdued, more like they were before chaos had been introduced. This is not surprising to anyone who studies human behavior; humans are adaptive, and children are resilient. Many may assume that she simply adjusted to what was going on around her. I agree with this viewpoint; it works. In fact, it was a biological given of human behavior that I had been counting on to kick in at the proper time. It didn't seem fair to leave her to the routine. She might still be doing the same things when she was middle aged that she was doing in these childhood years, and she would miss so much. Life isn't like that. Life in our world was chaotic, so I chose chaos as the route for Jessica.

Chaos is the perfect name for it. There is no rhyme or reason to much in our lives. Scheduled chaos is what I created. For instance, one night she might have dinner at the table as usual, but the next we might eat a picnic in the backyard, in the car looking out at the lake, or in my room watching a movie. It was different from the day before, both in location and by at least 15 minutes on the clock. She might be allowed to stay up a little later, or she might be put to bed early. We might brush our teeth before the bath, or after. As long as everything gets done, it shouldn't matter in what order it happens.

Here is an illustration as an introduction to the chaos regimen. Anyone can do it. It is not difficult. I simply made a schedule of times. At first, I printed one off on my computer every month for every task that I needed to schedule. I had one sheet for the bedtimes, one for the bath times, one for the dinnertimes, and so on.

As a student, I carried with me an academic planner from the college bookstore where I worked. I had grown accustomed to the format of having a half page to write my schedule on, but eventually I moved on to a full-page Franklin planner. This became the place where I wrote the dinnertimes, bath times and bedtimes. In between, I would throw in brushing teeth and random story times and other chaotic additions, so that every day held many surprises. In addition, we had therapy goals to attend to each and every day. These were not written down on my planner. I would allow Jessica to go to her room, and at some point one of the team members or I would show up, unannounced, to start therapy time with her. At other times, I would simply go in to play with her or talk to her. It was hard work, but very rewarding.

The three events I "scheduled with chaos," dinnertime, bath time, and bedtime, were chosen strategically. That is, these three events happen every night, or should happen every night. You must eat, and you must sleep. A child should bathe every night, but most parents battle kids on the spectrum when it comes to hygiene. Pick your battles as you can handle them. You know your child better than anyone.

The battle to get Jessica to take a bath lasted for more than a year. I finally discovered the trick when I noticed that she had become somewhat attached to some bath toys. The toys were only allowed in the bathroom, so I used them to entice her into the tub. Even then, she would resist; and washing her hair was nothing short of a fiasco.

Bedtime was a terrible fight for a while, too. For about six months she would continue to get up, over and over again; she would play in her room quietly, and even come out as if it were morning. She ended up staying awake until 11:00 p.m. or so every night. This worried me for a while, but I began waking her very early in the morning in an attempt to "reset her clock." We spent time in the morning before kindergarten making pancakes together and then cleaning up the mess. (We made more mess than pancakes.)

Because of these events, and the scheduling of chaos, and the mindset that everything is therapy for the individual on the Autism Spectrum, every moment became a teaching moment. If your child has to take a bath BEFORE dinner, or finish his homework AFTER taking his bath, is that really the end of the world? Being able to switch tasks flawlessly is a good goal. It's good practice. Praising your child for doing something simple like that is a great self-esteem builder. Celebrate the little steps, I say!

Bed, bath, and dinnertime are just the three events I chose to put on my planner (it is impossible to mess about with kids' school routines, for example). I did not post the "routine." On some days I announced when we were going home what time dinner would be served, if Jessica asked me. Especially, if she was having a bad day, she would need the reassurance of knowing what would be happening later and, therefore, asked. I did not let her look at my planner. Most of the time, she would find out what was happening as it was happening. For example, I would call her name and tell her that it was time for her to take her bath. She might resist, but she would start preparing to take her bath. I told her once, and then I went in to help her. Sometimes it was before dinner; sometimes after dinner. She never knew. This element of surprise was essential to the evening's successful therapy session. However, I did announce what time dinner was being served, as dinner was being served every night, so that she could hear and keep in her mind that it was different from last night. When she did not have a tantrum or react adversely to these changes, she was praised. If we had a somewhat peaceful dinner, she would be praised: "I am so proud of you for behaving so nicely, Jessica. It makes me want to take you places with me. Thank you for such nice manners!"

Other families may have other items that they'd like to schedule chaos with. Certainly, the regimen can be used with anything that is part of the everyday routine, or with anything that is relatively routine in your life. You pick your times out, at random – by using a chart like the following.

Sample Time Chart

100 101 102 103 104 105 106 107 108 109 110 111 112 113 114

115 116 117 118 119 120 121 122 123 124 125 126 127 128 129

130 131 132 133 134 135 136 137 138 139 140 141 142 143 144

145 146 147 148 149 150 151 152 153 154 155 156 157 158 159

200 201 202 203 204 205 206 207 208 209 210 211 212 213 214

215 216 217 218 219 220 221 222 223 224 225 226 227 228 229

230 231 232 233 234 235 236 237 238 239 240 241 242 243 244

245 246 247 248 249 250 251 252 253 254 255 256 257 258 259

300 301 302 303 304 305 306 307 308 309 310 311 312 313 314

315 316 317 318 319 320 321 322 323 324 325 326 327 328 329

330 331 332 333 334 335 336 337 338 339 340 341 342 343 344

345 346 347 348 349 350 351 352 353 354 355 356 357 358 359

400 401 402 403 404 405 406 407 408 409 410 411 412 413 414

415 416 417 418 419 420 421 422 423 424 425 426 427 428 429

430 431 432 433 434 435 436 437 438 439 440 441 442 443 444

445 446 447 448 449 450 451 452 453 454 455 456 457 458 459

500 501 502 503 504 505 506 507 508 509 510 511 512 513 514
515 516 517 518 519 520 **521** 522 523 524 525 **526** 527 528 529
530 531 532 533 **534** 535 536 537 **538** 539 540 541 542 **543** 544
545 546 **547** 548 549 **550** 551 552 553 554 555 556 **557** 558 559

600 601 **602** 603 604 605 606 **607** 608 609 **610** 611 612 613 614
615 616 **617** 618 619 620 **621** 622 623 **624** 625 **626** 627 628 **629**
630 **631** 632 633 **634** 635 636 637 **638** 639 640 **641** 642 643 644
645 646 647 648 **649** 650 651 **652** 653 654 655 656 **657** 658 659

700 701 **702** 703 704 **705** 706 707 708 **709** 710 711 712 **713** 714
715 716 717 718 719 720 721 722 723 724 725 726 727 728 729
730 731 732 733 734 735 736 737 738 739 740 741 742 743 744
745 746 747 748 749 750 751 752 753 754 755 756 757 758 759

800 801 802 803 804 805 806 807 808 809 810 811 812 813 814
815 816 817 818 819 820 821 822 823 824 825 826 827 828 829
830 831 832 833 834 835 836 837 838 839 840 841 842 843 844
845 846 847 848 849 850 851 852 853 854 855 856 857 858 859

900 901 902 903 904 905 906 907 908 909 910 911 912 913 914
915 916 917 918 919 920 921 922 923 924 925 926 927 928 929
930 931 932 933 934 935 936 937 938 939 940 941 942 943 944
945 946 947 948 949 950 951 952 953 954 955 956 957 958 959

1000 1001 1002 1003 1004 1005 1006 1007 1008 1009 1010 1011 1012 1013 1014

1015 1016 1017 1018 1019 1020 1021 1022 1023 1024 1025 1026 1027 1028 1029

1030 1031 1032 1033 1034 1035 1036 1037 1038 1039 1040 1041 1042 1043 1044

1045 1046 1047 1048 1049 1050 1051 1052 1053 1054 1055 1056 1057 1058 1059

1100 1101 1102 1103 1104 1105 1106 1107 1108 1109 1110 1111 1112 1113 1114

1115 1116 1117 1118 1119 1120 1121 1122 1123 1124 1125 1126 1127 1128 1129

1130 1131 1132 1133 1134 1135 1136 1137 1138 1139 1140 1141 1142 1143 1144

1145 1146 1147 1148 1149 1150 1151 1152 1153 1154 1155 1156 1157 1158 1159

1200 1201 1202 1203 1204 1205 1206 1207 1208 1209 1210 1211 1212 1213 1214

1215 1216 1217 1218 1219 1220 1221 1222 1223 1224 1225 1226 1227 1228 1229

1230 1231 1232 1233 1234 1235 1236 1237 1238 1239 1240 1241 1242 1243 1244

1245 1246 1247 1248 1249 1250 1251 1252 1253 1254 1255 1256 1257 1258 1259

Another effective way to use this system is to use different-colored markers or highlighters to indicate times scheduled for dinner, for bath time, or bedtime, etc. Develop a system that works well for you. Be forewarned, however, that if you use the same times every month, the child may soon discover that "bedtime on the 15th of the month will be at 9:27 p.m." Then, you will have a new routine to break!

The name of the game here is scheduled chaos. Pick times randomly. For example, you should have 30 different dinnertimes for the month of September, each at least 9-15 minutes different from the night before. (Fifteen minutes is best, but beginning with nine may be an easier transition for some items in a child's routine.) In addition, your goal should include several opportunities to change the eating venue: in the living room on TV trays, picnic style in another room of the house, in the backyard, or in the park, in the car, or at a friend's house. I have highlighted an example of 30 dinnertimes to get you started. Bon appetit!

It needs to be "okay" to do things in different orders. We should learn to go with the natural flow around us. Otherwise, we never have any fun and are always upset with how things are going. My children on the Autism Spectrum became easygoing, and are able to manage outside agendas very effectively, and I believe that it is because of this scheduled chaos regimen that broke the routine that they had otherwise set for themselves.

For me, as for many parents of children on the Autism Spectrum, going out in public was a harrowing experience. Jessica was a toddler who was often hard to handle. I remember the days before I had children of my own talking negatively about parents who put leashes and harnesses on their kids. I spoke with such self-righteous abandon about how such things were meant for dogs, and that if people couldn't control their children, perhaps they shouldn't have them at all. Ahhhh … the ignorance of youth.

Out of necessity I took Jessica to the grocery store one afternoon before her fourth birthday. I had to steer the cart with one hand and keep one arm around her to keep her in the cart. In the pickle and peanut butter aisle, she went berserk. She started with some gentle flapping and squealing to let me know she wanted to get out of the seat, and then she struck out at me, kicking and screaming. Her body went rigid, and she pushed upwards with her arms with such force that it nearly launched her little body out of the cart. When I grabbed her, she proceeded to bang her head against mine, and kick me with her legs. I knelt to get better leverage on the floor, but the episode caught her so quickly, and the emotional storm blew in with such force, that it was just a few moments before I was lying with her on the floor, bracing her arms and legs, and taking the full blows of her head against my chin and chest to prevent her from hurting her head against the floor or the shelving. Not surprisingly, we drew a crowd of onlookers. After two or three minutes, the wildness in her eyes subsided, and I was finally able to release her. We were a mess. She had busted my bottom lip against my teeth with her head, and had my blood in her hair. I dug into my purse to get some tissues to clean up the tears and the blood, and the smeared mascara.

Then I put her back into the cart. I still had to get milk and eggs and detergent, and there was nobody to help me. I remember feeling angry. I was angry at the people who had watched helplessly as we endured the storm, and said nothing. I was angry at the lady in front of me at the checkout counter, who chatted with her seemingly normal toddler about his choice of breakfast cereal. I was angry because of the questioning looks from the manager in the glass booth at the customer service desk as he surveyed me and the stains on my shirt from the floor of aisle #3 and the blood from my lip, then looked to my giggling and babbling filthy child in the cart, and her matted bloody mass of blonde hair. He exchanged a knowing glance with the security officer, and that made me angrier. What could anybody know about it?

I unloaded my cart, practically throwing the items into a pile on the conveyor belt. The teenager at the register smiled at me and asked, "How are you doing today, ma'am?" I was so angry and exhausted I could barely move my lips. "Fine," I whispered, in a voice that was barely audible. I left Jessica in the cart while I wrote my check, with one arm around her middle in case she decided to bolt again, and then lifted her out of the cart. She screamed in protest, not wanting to leave now. I needed both hands for the groceries, so I clipped my wrist strap to the back of the full chest harness Jessica was wearing. As I did so, I realized how pitiful the two of us must have looked. I felt something rising in my chest, choking me. I stopped and looked over my shoulder to make eye contact with a dozen pairs of eyes that were sizing us up. Then, I loaded up one hand with the plastic bags, and the other with the laundry detergent, and set off for the car.

Once outside, Jessica would jump and try to run out into traffic, so the harness was essential. She took the end of it and occasionally slipped her arm through like it was a bracelet, and once we were walking side by side, she was content to go along with me.

That "something" in my chest that was choking me doesn't have a name. It's some kind of an emotion. It's related to grief, and at times it's kind of like rage. It holds hands with depression at times, but it sets your chin defiantly against the world, and puts a mask over your face so the tears don't spill when you need to hold them back. It's a feeling that lets you smile even though your heart is breaking over and over and over again. It gives you the strength of a hundred armies. You can walk 10 miles without water or proper shoes (with a child on your back to boot). It's a feeling that is lower than desperation, and one that gets you out of bed every day and will never let you give up, all at the same time. There isn't a word in our language for that feeling, but when a dozen or so people are watching you and wondering what could be wrong with your family, it will choke you up sometimes.

Episodes like this will build up in your life, and from time to time you need a way to release some of your feelings, whatever they are. Whenever I had the opportunity, I would take Jessica to the Outer Banks near Kitty Hawk. It was a three-hour drive from where we lived. Because of Jessica's inability to control her volume levels, and because I was unable to leave her in a nursery, I was unable to go to church with any regularity, so we did not have a church home. Thus, I would take her to the Outer Banks on many Sundays. There, with a constant wind off the ocean, her shrieking and screaming mixed with the singing of the gulls, which sometimes masked it completely.

I found solace in the dunes, because although there are many tourists in the area, the usual places are the beach, the lighthouses, or the Wright Brothers monument. Jessica and I would walk at a comfortable distance from the tourist traffic. Most times, we were alone. I could unhook the harness and "let her fly." She would take off running, babbling away. I could keep a close eye on her, and there was nobody to bother us or hear me scream. And scream I did. I threw back my head and wailed on several occasions. I wept and pounded my fists on the sand. Afterwards, I generally felt much better. Jessica would giggle and run in circles around me, and I would collect myself, chastise myself for giving in to self-pity, anger, or whatever destructive feeling got me to that point, and then I would get up and join her in some game. When she was ready to sleep, I often laid her over my shoulder and walked through the Wright Brothers exhibit. I had always been inspired by them, and was glad for the opportunity to walk the same grounds so many years later.

It was during one of these trips that I read part of an address that Wilbur Wright gave in Chicago, to the Western Society of Engineers on September 18, 1901. He said: "If you are looking for perfect safety, you will do well to sit on a fence and watch the birds; but if you really wish to learn, you must mount a machine and become acquainted with its tricks by actual trial."

I knew exactly what he meant. The helpless onlookers who were making me so angry were birdwatching. I was trying to handle something I didn't know anything about. I was learning, by trial and error, the things that I must do in order to help Jessica succeed in life. I needed to be willing to mount my machine and risk everything. Wilbur Wright was willing to risk his life, and willing to show the world where he failed as well as where he succeeded. If he hadn't, we would never have flown. To use my daughter as a "guinea pig" and go on hunches to see what worked was pretty risky. It made me sick to think of it, but there was everything to gain if we succeeded.

The results of introducing chaos? A year later, we were able to stop at the grocery store on the way home from daycare if necessary and browse if we wanted to, without the fear of her tiring and having an episode. We could eat out in public. She would remain in her car seat without restraint from an adult. The biggest freedom was the ability to say to her, "Wait just a second. We have to do this first, and then we will go," or to be able to answer a ringing telephone on the way out the door.

This seems as if it were very simple. It was not at all simple. I did not succeed in everything that I tried, but I kept trying. Every day was a new day, and a new challenge. The days were grueling. Everyone who lives with challenges knows what I am referring to when I say that days can be grueling: It takes an extraordinary amount of time to get dressed every morning, because the clothes may be the wrong color, or they may be tied to something that the child has dreamed about and cannot express. It may trigger an episode. The episode may set the mood for the rest of the morning, or for the rest of the day. Hygiene is a constant issue. Food is an ever-present battle. Then, figure in the things that go amiss. Every once in a while, a child will trip, stumble, and fall down, which is an interruption in his pattern of walking. If the child is injured, even if it is just a scrape, it can be a tremendous blow.

These days, Jessica and I are no longer alone. She has two brothers, Alex and Averie, in the home with her now, thanks to my husband, Steve. The youngest, Averie, is also on the Autism Spectrum. He fell up the stairs one day going into a friend's home and skinned his shin slightly. It was 20 minutes before he felt able to stand again on his own power. In the meantime, the screaming was such that you would have thought he had broken his leg. Of course, these things are painful and should be acknowledged. The response was one you would expect to see from a toddler. But Averie was 8 years old.

I use this example because life happens, and it is sometimes difficult to manage. Teaching all three of my kids various social skills has significantly decreased the frequency of these episodes, but the more significant changes in behavior have come from casting off the routine, and concentrating on the patterns that emerged on the matrix.

Parents know their children better than anyone. I know my Jessica. I know her limits. I pushed the envelope daily with her, but I didn't push her too hard. She wouldn't doubt that I loved her. She wouldn't be neglected or deprived of love, food, warmth, or safety. Occasionally, she was deprived of immediate gratification. This was most likely a positive thing. In my opinion, most of the rest of us would have been a lot better off if some of our gratification demands had been denied at times.

Like the rest of the world, Jessica learned to wait. The Autistic tendency is that it demands its own way, on its own schedule. The world we live in doesn't function that way. She would never be prepared to live in it, if I allowed her to demand her own way on her own schedule. I decided to apply chaos theory to shake things up, and then to introduce behavior modification to further wake things up. I devoted every fiber of my being to her. All I really did, fundamentally, was raise the bar and demand that she raise her own expectations of herself. What I learned was that when I raised that bar, she met it. I began to wonder if one day she would question me and ask if I kept that bar too low, so I removed it altogether.

Ten years later, she wonders why I didn't set that bar a little higher in the beginning. "Hey, it took me a little while to catch on," I'd say! I tell her constantly that I am proud of how much courage it takes for her to live her life. I know how much courage it takes to live mine. With behavior modification, or therapy that uses conditioning and reinforcement, you are constantly under fire, but we get to that soon enough.

CHAPTER FOUR

Behavior Modification Therapy

"Finding Triggers and Chasing Monsters"

B ehavior modification. The words send shivers down the spines of many, sometimes even conjuring up images of torture. Why, then, would I choose this form of therapy for my young daughter? To begin answering this question, I need to define two words: *assimilation* and *accommodation*.

Both assimilation and accommodation refer to stages of cognitive development. Assimilation is the ability to change the environment to meet your needs. Experiences are accepted only when they fit into what is already known; that is to say, we can only process new ideas by attempting to fit them into our old ideas. For instance, children learn to play soccer because they already know how to run and to kick a ball.

Accommodation is the opposite. It refers to accepting new experiences and ideas, regardless of how different they are from what we already know or have experienced in the past. In this form of cognitive development, every experience is a new one, regardless of how similar it is to previous ones.

When a person encounters a new experience, assimilation and accommodation usually occur at the same time. The patterns of thinking are changed at the same time that known skills are being called upon to help with the new skill. It's a relatively even process.

With some children on the Autism Spectrum, the scales are unbalanced. Jessica, like many kids on the Spectrum was intent on pure, unbridled assimilation. She was completely focused on making the world around her work only for her. She would never have recognized a need to learn any new skills. She was isolated in the void of her own creation.

Behavior modification in her case, therefore, was about balancing that scale. With conditioning as the major goal, I set about making her a bit more accommodating. She needed new experiences of every kind. Most of all, she needed to be experiencing the same things that others in her peer group were experiencing and processing.

I made a list, with the help of the therapists and other parents, and information from sources on child development. I also went on a sort of field trip to an elementary school and observed young children and what they did. I asked teachers, parents and friends about their children, and about their likes and dislikes. This list became a set of goals … with no set schedule, of course!

Here is a list that I have compiled. These are "benchmarks" for the ages listed. I have listed ages 2-5 for the purposes of early detection of developmental delay. There are some great sources available on the web. One of the best current sources that I found was the National Network for Child Care at Iowa State University (www.nncc.org). Almost all of the items on my lists were on those lists as well as many more!

A typical 2-year-old:

Climbs up/down stairs	Plays in sand with toys
Stacks blocks 4 or 5 high	Scribbles with crayons
Can use a spoon	"I can do it myself!"
Imitates parents	Engages in dress-up play
Pretends with phone	Kisses and hugs
Not aggressive but …	Hits another child in the face when angry
Is shy around strangers	Loves mirrors
Likes mud	Understands sharing
Can't copy artwork	Is attached to caregivers

A typical 3-year-old:

Listens to books	Likes fairy tales
Able to tell stories	Can sing songs
Sleeps through night	Self-feeds
Dresses self	Catches balls
Starts toileting	Knows concept of "now/later"
Names colors of red, blue, yellow and green	Kicks a ball
Knows shapes of circle and square	Stacks up to 7 blocks
Can follow directions at preschool/share, etc	Likes play-dough
Can play the "which of these things is not like the others" game	Can name animals and some body parts
Knows his name and his age	Washes hands
Understands "why/when who/where"	Hops on one foot
Knows difference between girls and boys	Seeks approval of parents
Likes jokes	Talks to puppets
Likes to color in coloring books	Knows happy/sad/angry

A typical 4-year-old:

Uses eating utensils to feed self	Pedals a tricycle
Runs and jumps around things easily	Skips
Dresses self	Bathes and washes
Brushes teeth	Laces shoes (not tie)
Counts to seven	Puts things in simple order
Recognizes familiar words (stop signs, etc.)	Recognizes letters in alphabet
Understands superlatives (biggest, smallest, same, most)	Communicates in complete sentences
Stacks 10 blocks	Makes animals out of play-dough
Makes bead necklaces	Turns somersaults
Remembers songs	Likes playing "Follow the Leader"
Knows name/address/phone number	Knows 6 to 8 colors and 3 shapes
Can remember what happened yesterday	Asks "why why why why why??????"
Talks all the time	Changes game rules
Lies to get out of trouble	Tattles
Throws fits to get own way	Engages in elaborate pretending
Can share, but girls can be bossy	Is afraid of the dark, monsters, ghosts

A typical 5-year-old:

Uses scissors	Can catch a ball that is bouncy
Skips well	Jumps rope
Makes up stories	Can trace pictures
Remembers jokes	Understands how to categorize objects
Understands meanings of prepositions (under, over, after, before, etc.)	Understands some family relationships (brother/sister, aunt/uncle)
Collects things	Likes to be alone sometimes
Likes to give presents	Acts "grown up"
Shows jealousy	Tests physical strength
May lose interest in tricycle, or act ready to move up to a two-wheeler	Reasons out why he wants something using the word "because"
Is afraid of firecrackers/loud noises in general	Mixes up fantasy and reality
Can play independently	Likes games such as "Simon Says" and "Hokey Pokey"

Behavior modification is an area of great controversy. My stance is starkly simple. I am a supporter. However, I agree that it does not work for every circumstance. I recognize that each person must be dealt with on an individual basis. Just like you don't treat every cancer patient with chemotherapy, you don't treat every person on the Autism Spectrum with behavior modification. Some respond to it; others do not. Further, therapy is often uncomfortable. Therapy can be painful from time to time. Not physically painful in this instance. It is emotionally painful, as emotionally painful as psychotherapy because you are reconditioning the body's auto-response system.

To illustrate, imagine that you're drinking cocoa. The cocoa is hot, and it burns your tongue; you start to cry. I wait with you until you stop crying. I give you another cup. It isn't as hot as the first one. It burns a little still, and you don't want it, because you think all cocoa is going to burn you. Now you are mad; you start to cry because you are mad. I wait with you until you stop crying. I am patient. We talk some more. I give you another cup. This one is really good. You like the cocoa. We have a good talk. It is a good session.

You guessed it. All three cups were the same temperature. This is an illustration of simple conditioning. At the end of the session, I tell you the secret and say that you have really accomplished something by being able to overcome that. (Please know that I didn't burn Jessica's tongue with cocoa.) Many individuals with Autism Spectrum Disorders have a sensitivity to hot and cold liquids, claiming that they are too hot or too cold when they are at nearly room temperature. Jessica had a similar problem. By using something akin to the above scenario, I gradually increased the temperature of the cocoa. She orders it in restaurants now, without incident, and drinks any variety or brand, with or without marshmallows. She especially likes being able to go to the concession stand with her friends at ball games during cold weather and order it.

It might be beneficial to add here that many times, a person with Autism acts out in undesirable ways because she is unable to communicate pain or an intense dislike of certain stimuli. When I was doing my initial reading on pervasive developmental disorders, I checked a book out of the library about the Lovaas method of aversive behavior modification. It outlined some fairly strong techniques, and some that seemed to be fairly painful at times, in teaching persons with Autism what behaviors were undesirable. I don't believe in causing physical pain!

Many people on the Autism Spectrum have difficulty with pain perception. Information from the senses crosses paths, and this combined with oversensitivity can mean that they may process sensations in unusual ways. Transitions of any kind, the breaks in the routine, can also be extremely uncomfortable or distressing. In some instances, it may seem as if the individual on the Autism Spectrum perceives these transitions as physical pain.

I would never intentionally cause my child physical pain. However, I see a genuine need for therapy. I saw immediate results with behavior modification. The name of Lovaas is synonymous with an expert in behavior modification, and for good reason. The methods I read of were from the late 60s and early 70s, and since that time, changes have prompted the Lovaas program into more adaptive treatments of Autism than just pure behavior modification.

I have to stop and remind all free-thinking individuals that kids with Autism are kids first, and individuals with Autism second. If you are not going to allow your child without Autism to jump on the kitchen table because it is an inappropriate behavior, you should teach your child with

Autism the same rule. Failure to do so is doing that child a social disservice. I fully recognize that the child with Autism may not acknowledge that the rules apply to him. He may have no understanding of the rules, but the rules should be taught nonetheless. Your children are listening, and it is okay for you to administer some loving discipline.

You cannot love your kids too much, or be too fair with them. When I was pointing out inappropriate behaviors and laying out the ground rules, it helped me to be able to say to Jessica, "Listen, I know you are doing your very best and I am so proud of you. I need you to work on something for me. When someone is talking on the phone, it is not polite to interrupt by screaming or talking. If you see me on the phone, I would like it if you would try to wait until I am done talking and hang up before you talk to me. Today, you interrupted me four times when I was talking. I was talking to my friend so it was not a problem, and I am not angry today. Next time, it might upset me if I am talking to a stranger, so I want you to work on that. If you really need me, like there's an emergency, then it's always okay to interrupt. I know that you may forget sometimes, but do your best."

Depending on the noise or her attention level, I might ask Jessica to repeat a little of what I said to be sure she understood. The talks took between 30 seconds and 1 minute. Then the matter was to be dropped by us both, and neither of us would talk about it again unless we had some questions later. That way, she wouldn't have to worry about being in trouble about it any further. I would smile and say thank you for listening. I always ended by saying "I love you." The next time she interrupted, I reminded her of the conversation, and then told her that the next time she interrupted would bring consequences, but I would not yell or be angry. Once, when I was able to have a conversation on the telephone and she did not interrupt, I rewarded her with a treat. She was in another room, probably unaware that I had been on the phone at all, but she was surprised and delighted by the treat, and pleased with herself for being such a good helper by not interrupting. I had "caught her being good," an important strategy when using behavior management.

The majority of behavior management techniques (BMT) can be incorporated into an applied behavior analysis, or ABA, regimen and individualized for each child. In fact, that's the only way BMT is effective. It must seem unusual to try to reason with a child bucking on the floor, or shrieking and flapping. I would set a wiggling, jabbering toddler down on a bench, who would go rigid at my touch, and proceed to speak calmly and intelligently to her as she babbled and stared past my head into space.

But she was listening. I wonder what might have happened if I hadn't said anything!

I had a great many people question why I attempted to reason with Jessica, implying that it wasn't possible for her to reason at my level. Perhaps, I acknowledged, but if she could understand me at all, then not trying to reach her was a complete waste of time.

I have stated my case for behavior modification, and with therapy in general. Therapy is a necessity. You would not stop therapy when it is needed. You would not stop stretching the legs of a child suffering from a debilitating physical condition, or who had been burned, because she cried from the physical pain. You would not stop cancer treatment because it made the patient sick. My child cried. She was sometimes upset to the point that it made her sick. I was sick, too. She would cry herself to sleep. Then I would cry myself to sleep. It was not an easy beginning. But I believed in the progress that we were making.

This was where we began to see changes – almost like miracles – start happening.

We went to register Jessica for kindergarten at the local public school. We had her first IEP meeting. She was present and banging her head. I was told that she would have to wear a helmet. When she reached a certain weight, her helmet would have to have a mouthpiece also, so that it would protect her tongue. I was devastated. My worst fears had come true.

I left the school, deciding on the way home that Jessica would attend private kindergarten. So I began researching the private schools in the area, and looking for the right teacher. After some searching, I found a teacher with 25 years' experience, and a classroom with only 20 kids. The Guy School was a quiet little school with excellent standards. I explained to the headmaster that Jessica was a little developmentally delayed and that she had Autism, but that for a while I didn't believe she needed any special accommodations. He understood the need to put her in a general education classroom, and placed her in a class with a very experienced teacher. She started kindergarten on time with her peers, without a helmet and mouthgear – and for the time being, without an IEP.

Shortly after she started school, I saw Jessica outside on the ground under our swing set, banging her head on the ground. I don't remember who was on the phone with me. I don't remember if I hung up the phone or not, but I immediately opened the sliding glass door and walked over to where she was sitting. I braced her hips on either side with my knees and shins. I put my hands on either side of her head and restrained her, holding her head to the ground. I did not hurt her, I just held her.

She screamed and clawed at my hands. She bucked and kicked. After a few minutes, she lay there and sobbed, and I started talking to her. Tears ran down my face, but I kept talking. "Jessica, I'm your mommy and I love you so much, but if you bang your head, you're are going to hurt yourself. I can't let you hurt yourself, so banging your head is against the rules. Do you understand the rules?" I said this, and things like this, over and over again, for 15 minutes. I know it was 15 minutes because I was timing myself. My legs went to sleep. I was aching everywhere. My tears ran down my cheeks and fell into her hair. I half expected the authorities to show up because a neighbor might have called to report "some crazy lady in the backyard strangling a child under a swing set." I just kept watching Jessica. She stopped crying and turned her eyes back at me, and I was suddenly aware that she was listening to me. I had her attention. I kept repeating those words. "Do you understand me, Jessica?" And it came, "Yes, Mommy." Clear as a bell. I let go immediately.

She sat up and looked at me. "I love you so much," I said. She just got up and went in the house, as if nothing had happened.

I was rattled to my core. I sat there for a few minutes, shaking. From that day on, she has never hit her head on anything. As a result, she never wore a helmet or headgear of any kind at school. I had a hard time getting to my feet and walking back inside the house that afternoon, I had the same feeling that something significant had occurred as I did the afternoon when she had said "bottle." Again, I had pushed the envelope. She had responded. It was about finding the right trigger.

It seemed that sticking to the house rules was working; at least to some extent. Jessica was extremely rule-oriented. We made a list of house rules, and she did her best to abide by them. Slowly, we added behaviors to the list. We took one behavior at a time, and carefully worked on it, and then gradually added it to the list. Then, we would start on something else. Everyone in our life heard my mantra: "Pick your battles!" As I let her rock and babble, they would frown and shake their heads at me, while I explained that we were working on getting her to stop turning in circles. But before too long, Jessica would be heard to say "No spinning allowed," and we would be on to the next behavior. Then the next, and the next, and the next. While we worked on one behavior, nothing was said about any of the others, but there was lots and lots of praise for all work done on the behavior she was working on eliminating!

If one Autistic behavior could be eliminated, it stood to reason that others could be eliminated as well, if the correct trigger could be identified. The next behavior that I focused on was a tic that Jessica had with her hand. She would fold her fingers at the first knuckle and hold her hand at the level of her face, and rotate it in an odd manner. At times it appeared as if she were balancing an imaginary tray on that hand, and at other times, it looked as if she were holding an invisible ball, but always, she would twirl her wrist about in that odd way. She looked off into space, past her hand; she was watching the hand out of the corner of her eye.

In an effort to change her behavior, I began to look for things to put into her hand. I looked for things that she would otherwise not be allowed to have. Of course, she would be supervised. The first time I handed her a spatula from the kitchen drawer because we happened to be in the kitchen. It wasn't effective. She dropped it. I noticed her a few minutes later with her hand twisting, I now put my car keys into her hand. She wasn't impressed. Down went my keys, but she had held onto them for a few seconds, and had stopped babbling, so I knew it had jolted her a bit.

About an hour later, I got my next chance. I noticed the hand twisting. I took out my earring and placed it into her hand. Jessica stopped twisting. Her hand closed around the earring. Then something amazing happened. She grabbed the earring with the other hand, and then went in for a look with both eyes. She focused! Immediately I went for it. I talked for a good 10 minutes to her about that earring. We interacted. It was so simple, but it was an invitation for her to come out of The Void.

When she lost interest and drifted away again, I put the earring back into my ear. Then I got a shoebox and began collecting things that she might be interested in. Sewing scissors, beads, pretty rocks, nail clippers, figurines, Christmas ornaments, foreign coins, paper dolls, jewelry of all kinds, buttons, rocks, shells, and other things that I could find around the house. All of the things were small and fragile, unsuitable for young children, things you would take away from children, shiny things and fun things to play with.

Every day I would put some of these things into my pocket. They were my invitations for her to come out of The Void. She became accustomed to the way that it worked. Over time, she began not to move the hand any more, but she would hold it still and wait for me to put something in it. Finally, I began to be able to just touch the palm of her hand and give her a verbal cue to put it down. At this point, I made it a rule. Like the headbanging, I said that it was against the rules. I told her that I would understand if she forgot for a little while, but that I would help her to remember by touching her hand and reminding her. Eventually, the tic was eliminated. By the time she finished kindergarten, she no longer demonstrated that behavior at all.

In the title of this chapter, I mentioned chasing monsters. One such monster was self-stimulation. Children with Autism bang their heads, spin objects, or flail, because they are self-stimulating. They are creating their environments, a sort of comfort zone. It seems unreasonable that banging one's head could be comforting. However, when you consider that the rest of the world is completely out of control and you cannot communicate your wants and needs, but you have found that you CAN control the zone immediately around you, then who is to judge what is comforting to another person? The Autistic person becomes accustomed to the monotonous thumping of the headbanging, the gentle rocking back and forth, the sound of it, the feel of it; it is hypnotic. It's a sort of trance. It is self-stimulating.

The difficulty that I encountered trying to eliminate one self-stimulatory behavior was that it immediately manifested in another form of self-stimulatory behavior. For example, when I eliminated the headbanging, Jessica's rocking back and forth in a fetal position increased dramatically. I did not immediately make this an issue. I picked another battle. I decided that rocking was easier for her to handle on the immediate front than wearing a helmet.

Later, as Jessica progressed, we gradually eliminated the rocking as well. I didn't worry too much about one behavior manifesting or "replacing" another. She was doing the best she could to cope with the constant change. Every time I saw a behavior I wished to eliminate, I pushed crayons into her hands and we went for the artistic side of things. Many people escape into their art, and she seemed to enjoy being creative. Therefore, when she was found to be in a self-stimulatory state, she was immediately redirected.

Sometimes redirection is successful and sometimes it is not. As creative as we humans are, there is only so much you can do before you realize that you are still upset and dive right back into self-destructive, or worse yet, self-mutilating behavior. This is one of those gray areas where other parents, teachers, paraprofessionals, and others question me, saying things like, "What gives you the right to deprive an Autistic child of her need for self-stimming? How DARE you!" Yes, I know. All individuals, whether on the Autism Spectrum or not, need a self-stimulatory "comfort" behavior. We all need to unwind. We all have felt that urge to bang our heads against the wall. As we dealt with the need to "self-stim," I would offer a pillow to Jessica for scrunching with her hands. We would focus our energies on scrunching instead of these other behaviors. She proved that she was able to retrain herself. Any stimulatory behavior that she engages in now is done privately. It has evolved to her rubbing her temples or rolling her shoulders when alone in her room, or relaxing in the shower when she feels the need to unwind or to stim. She also plays the piano. When she is very agitated, she takes deep breaths as in yoga. I will never pretend that I know what "normal" is, but it is my estimation these are all natural ways to handle stress and strain.

In addition, we worked a great deal on refocusing her stress into her art and her music. When she needs to self-stim, she is sometimes able to go to the piano instead. It sounds remarkably normalized, doesn't it? It is. I never expected her to do anything different; she's human. The fundamental thing that I did was to raise my level of expectation. I raised the bar. She rose to meet the challenge every time.

She has no limits. This does not mean that she will succeed in everything that she attempts to do. This does not mean that everything that I tried worked every time. We had plenty of heartbreaks. Being firm about what was expected was the determining factor. We learned about stress, identified what caused her stress, and talked about ways to handle stress – forget who it's acceptable to.

I must back up now and talk about implementing her therapy. I took time to explain the methods of discipline, to illustrate the levels of trust we built between us.

The therapy regimen was fairly easy to implement. Besides the therapy that Jessica received at school and through the Post Family Services on Fort Bragg, I enlisted the help of several students and friends at Methodist College, where I was a student. I lived in North Carolina, and all of our family was still in Arkansas, which made it difficult to form a support network. My team consisted of 9-13 people at any given time. They were friends, mostly, but some were working in the special education department and only worked with us for one semester. They came from every sort of background. They were a very multicultural bunch. With their help, I was able to have someone interacting with Jessica around the clock. It was important to me that it not always be me. I would be continuing with school and work, and she would have to continue to respond to clinicians. The more she could socialize with others, the better, I reasoned. It wasn't hard to teach the team to use the verbal cues I used to respond to Jessica. I would do the hardest work, what I referred to as bushwhacking, and they would follow my lead with support.

The regimen itself was rather flexible. Life skills were on the docket every day. Feeding herself without plastering the entire kitchen with food was an accomplishment; I was always hoping for improvement in this area. Being able to help her with the basics of oral hygiene without being bitten was always being worked on. Other areas included dressing herself, identifying colors and shapes, and of course, *Hooked on Phonics*!

Everything in the house had a sticky note on it, a label with the name of the object, in plain view. The therapists and I would point to these things at random times and say "Hey, look at that! It's a … (pause for

effect and point at the) … lamp!,", or "Wow, Jessica, look at the …
(pose like Vanna) … washing machine!" We were all in our own little
Sesame Street-meets-Mr. Rogers Neighborhood world. She would
look, sometimes, and, for a while we had no clue whether or not any of
it was sinking in.

Since Jessica loved Barbie, so the therapists played Barbie with her
almost constantly – I am happy to report a consistency here with most
other girls Jessica's age. There were naked Barbies everywhere. It made
some of the male members of the team a little uncomfortable. One of
them, who was very vocal about the naked-Barbie situation, requested
that we clothe the Barbies before his sessions with Jessica. I found this
hysterical. He was funny, and he was a very effective facilitator. Jessica
liked working with him a great deal.

Jessica loved Barbie, and Barbie dolls made our behavior modification
model highly effective. Parents need not worry that they can't attempt a
behavior modification therapy regimen of their own. They can! The
trick is finding the proper tool. Barbie was the catalyst for us. She was
so effective that Jessica responded to a regimen assembled by her parent, at the time somewhat untrained and lacking a college degree, and
facilitated by non-licensed practitioners. The argument that "Jessica
would respond to her mother, and to people that she knew and trusted,
more readily than she would to a school therapist or clinician" doesn't
work here, because with the exception of three members on the team,
Jessica had never met any of the team members, and they all proved to
be highly effective as well. They all worked with Barbie as much as I
did, and with the same level of effectiveness. It was the tool. Find your
trigger, your catalyst, your "Barbie," so to speak, and you've got it!

Barbie was an effective therapy tool, because we used her to model life
skills. In fact, she was used to model just about everything. She soon
was used to model appropriate speech. Jessica did not have words, so
the Barbies would talk to each other. Jessica watched them looking at
one another when they spoke … but I am getting ahead of myself.

Jessica Speaks: On What It Was Like in My Own Little World

Mom calls this "The Void" because it was a lot like being in darkness. Not to sound insane or anything, but it was truly like darkness. I would yearn for attention, and I wanted people to comfort me, because I felt alone. I was the only child in the house at the time.

Any time I got attention, it would make me uncomfortable. It would make me flinch. I would try to push them away. My body would get really stiff like a mannequin at the mall. I couldn't help it. It just happened. There were some times that I wanted comfort because I had a scary thought. I would end up in a corner rocking myself for comfort.

I was scared of things in my room because I was afraid that the dolls and pictures would come to life. I wasn't able to talk, so I couldn't tell my mom why I was scared. The thing I was most afraid of was dark places. Dark places had monsters and evil creatures in them, I thought. I wouldn't even wear black clothes because of this. Now I know better.

I was scared of a lot of things. I was scared of all the rides at Disney World. I understand now that being Autistic sometimes means that it's harder for me to try new things and overcome my fears. I rode all the rides anyway, and I tried a whole lot of new foods when we lived in Japan. I have had great adventures, and luckily for me, I know how to face my fears.

CHAPTER FIVE

The 3 L's of Discipline

"Love a Lot – Laugh a Lot – Learn a Lot"

As mentioned, Jessica understands house rules. Making something a house rule often was all it took to get the job done. Teams play by rules. A team can be made of two people, or it can consist of 10 or more. Whether it's 2, 10, 20 or more, when you're on a team you have to play by the rules. The rules apply to everybody, including you. Don't ask anything of your child that you are not prepared to do yourself. This is how you will earn your child's respect. Let the child see your sacrifice and your commitment. Don't make it a "do as I say and not as I do" environment. That breeds a "little-ownership-lotta-resentment" between kids and parents, whether or not you mean to or not. So go ahead and make your house rules. But if you say, for example, that only inside voices are to be used in the house, be prepared to stop yelling at your kid. Jessica trusted me already, but she respects what I did then, and she still respects what I do today.

In connection with our house rules, I had one set of repercussions for Jessica, and a different set for me. The repercussions – things/privileges we would lose – were based upon things that were important to each of us. On her list were the things that she liked to do, such as watching her videos, playing with Barbie, or having a favorite snack. If she stepped outside the boundaries of the house rules, together we would see what the repercussion for a given offense would be. It was fair. There was no yelling. We were diplomatic about it.

At first, she was unable to verbalize much about her understanding, and was unable to maintain eye contact. However, it was not difficult for me to realize that she understood fully what it was all about from her body language. Again, parents know their children better than anyone. It is fairly easy for a mother to distinguish the difference between infant cries. Hungry cries sound different than tired cries, and both are different from injured cries. If a parent is "in tune" with the child, it is rarely hard to determine whether the child has understood, at least to some degree, if what he or she has just done was right or wrong. I was careful to deal with issues immediately so that there was no time delay, and she was unable to prevent the distress from showing on her face. I was soon able to "read" some of her body movements. As she became more verbal, she indicated understanding verbally as we slowly eliminated the postures she had used to replace her lack of communication.

On my own list were things like taking a bubble bath, phone time talking to friends, and a favorite snack. I was also in the habit of listening to music in my room at night, and put that on the list as something to give up in the event that I yelled at Jessica for something that was not her fault.

All parents make mistakes. We are too easily pulled into the thinking of "I am the parent and what I say is the law around here. As long as you live in my house, you will obey my rules." I told Jessica from the beginning that she would have to trust that I knew a lot about how things should be because I was the parent and that is my job. I have always tried to be fair about her discipline. I never wanted her to perceive that I judge and jury over all that she did. I wanted to guide her, set the proper example, and then allow her the opportunity to choose. It sounds like an ideal situation. It has its flaws, like any disciplinary relationship, but overall it has worked beautifully.

This is not to say that I was never upset with her. On several occasions she acted like a regular kid, pushing and testing the limits like all kids will do. She was aware of the rules, and purposely stepped outside the limits. This began to happen when she was "coming out of her shell" a bit more at school. She would try to see how far she could push me, because at school she could get away with many things. They let her do whatever she wanted because of the Autism. Kids need limits; it is all part of the learning process. I never treated her differently because of the Autism. I treated her like a kid. Failure to discipline kid behavior is doing your child a disservice. To some degree, children figure out how to work people to their advantage. So when Jessica purposely stepped outside the rules, she knew that I was unhappy about it; however, I was willing to let her pay the penalties we had agreed upon for whatever transgression had occurred, and as long as she learned the behavioral lesson from the experience, I let it go. That was our agreement. If the behavior continued, the consequences would increase. Jessica understood why she was being disciplined, agreed somewhat with the need for the discipline, and had previously been involved in deciding what kind of penalty she would receive.

I refrain from using the word "punishment" whenever possible, because I feel that it is an extremely negative and overused term. If a child learns a lesson from being disciplined, then it is not punishment. A temporary restriction from a favorite activity or snack is only that – temporary – and should be used to illustrate a point related to the behavior that you want to see changed. Discipline is a good thing.

Helping your children determine when discipline is necessary is difficult sometimes. Tears are okay, and a little pouting is to be expected, but when your kids accept responsibility for their actions and learn from their disciplinary lessons, it is worth the effort.

One example of discipline in action is when Jessica lied to a teacher in kindergarten. The teacher was not her regular teacher, and she was extremely upset about the lie. She wrote me a note and sent it home with Jessica. It read:

"Jessica lied to me today after recess. You may want to discuss it with her. I told her that lying was a terrible act, and that it was unlikely that anyone would ever trust her if she continued to lie."

I was surprised and a little alarmed at reading the teacher's note. It must have been a terrible thing that Jessica had done, I reasoned, to prompt such a reaction. I immediately called Jessica into the living room to talk about it.

Me: "Jessica, how was school today?"

Jessica: "The teacher was to a meeting today. My teacher was green today." (She had been wearing a green sweater that day.)

Me: "You had a different teacher. Is that right or wrong? Tell me about the teacher."

Jessica: "My teacher was to a meeting so a different teacher was in my school. She didn't like me. She said I was a bad girl. She said Jessica lied to the teacher."

Me: "Did you lie to the teacher, Jessica?"

Jessica: "Yes."

Me: "Tell me about lying to the teacher."

Jessica: "I picked up the books."

Me: "Ooooo … Kaaaaay. You picked up the books. That's good. Did you get out the books?"

Jessica: "No."

Me: "Who got out the books?"

Jessica: "The boy."

Me: "The boy got out the books."

Jessica: "No."

Me: "OoooKAY. What did the boy do?"

Jessica: "The boy knocked down the books. I picked up the books."

Me: "And then what happened?"

Jessica: "The teacher was green."

Me: "Yes, I know. What did the green teacher do?"

Jessica: "She said Jessica was bad."

Me: "Yes, I know. What happened before that? Was it about the books?"

Jessica: "She said I knocked down the books. I said 'no' and then the green teacher said 'did you do that' and I said 'yes' and then she said I did that and I said 'no'."

Me: … (nodding my head, finally figuring out that the teacher had asked Jessica if she had knocked the books on the floor. She had answered yes, but was answering a different question. She was answering yes to 'did you pick up the books?' and was unable to communicate the difference to a woman who was substituting a kindergarten class. Ironically, now Jessica thought that she had done something wrong by picking up the books and thought she was bad, and was a liar.)

Her regular teacher and I agreed that the incident was not a big deal. At the time, Jessica was having a hard time distinguishing between fantasy and reality. The lie she told was compounded by the fact that the substitute teacher had scared her, and then directed a series of questions at her that confused Jessica. Jessica saw making up a lie as her means of escape.

Later, in elementary school, Jessica was caught in a true lie to her teacher. She had not studied for a test but did not want to disappoint one of her favorite teachers, so she lied and said she was sick and needed to go home. She went to the office, and I was called at work to come and get her. It was obvious that Jessica was not sick. I was relieved that she was not sick. However, I took her home and talked to her so that this did would not happen again.

Jessica realized the consequences of telling that lie when confronted. True to Autistic form, she told me what had happened, word for word. She told me what the teacher had said, and what she had said. When I asked her if what she had told the teacher was true, she said no. I asked her if she knew what made her tell the teacher something that was not true. She answered that she was afraid.

We talked briefly about telling the truth, and about how it was unacceptable to make up a story to escape a situation like that. I made an example of how she might feel if I told her a lie. I asked her if she thought she would be able to tell if I was telling the truth or not. She said that I always tell the truth. I asked her how she would feel if she found out that I told her a lie. She said that it would feel bad. I told her that when she made up stories like that, it was telling a lie, and it made other people feel bad, too. We both agreed that we wanted other people to feel good about Jessica, so telling lies wouldn't be a good thing.

Since it was the first time that she had been caught lying, I told her that we needed to make it part of our rules and decide what should happen if she did it again. We decided that lying was a big deal, so she would lose her video privileges completely if she lied. That is, for a certain number of days, she would have no videos. Every day that she told the truth after that would earn her one of her videos back of her choice. In other words, there was also a reward for positive behavior.

We only had to exercise this rule once.

Two weeks later, she lied again. This time to me. I knew that she was lying. Parents usually know when their kids are lying. It was fairly easy to tell. I asked her if she had finished all of her homework. She paused for a long time, rocked back and forth, humming and looking nervous, then finally said that she had. I waited a minute while I watched her rock back and forth and look at the opposite wall. I then asked her the same question again. Her response was more agitation and rocking; she waited for a little while before answering, but said yes again. I reminded her that we had been together all afternoon and that I knew she hadn't studied. I pointed out that I wasn't trying to trick her, but that my question was meant to serve as more of a reminder. I had been hoping that she would remember to read her assignment when I asked. Instead, she tried to get out of her responsibility of homework, which was not the right thing to do.

I didn't yell. I calmly pointed out that she had broken the rules. We went to the notebook where the rules were written down. Then calmly I took her into her room, and we packed up her videos. It was just a little lie, but it made my point beautifully. I kept her videos for two days. On the third day, I told her that she had done a great job at telling the truth, and that I was proud of how honest she was. Then I let her pick a video. The next day, she told me that she had been honest all day. I let her pick another video. This continued for several days.

At about day 10, she was terribly quiet about what had happened at school that day. When I pressed the issue, she admitted that she had not been honest all day. (It is important to point out that none of her so-called lies ever caused trouble for anyone else. The repercussions would have been much more severe if someone else had been affected.) It was obvious that Jessica felt bad about slipping. Again, I didn't yell. I expressed disappointment, but I encouraged her to continue working on changing her behavior. I told her that everybody messes up sometimes, and that nobody can be perfect all the time. I told her that she must fix the lie, and then she must move past it. As far as I was concerned, she was forgiven, but she had to make it right. Making it right meant telling the truth to the person she lied to, and surrendering the videos she had earned and starting over. She did this, grateful to have a solution to what was bothering her.

It seems a little dramatic to emphasize this so heavily. However, it was my hope that she would begin to see the defining lines between reality and the fantasy world she was creating for herself. It also brought another facet to our relationship: Since then Jessica has become very honest and reliable with information.

I have to point out that I wasn't perfect. I wore out sometimes. When a person is worn to a frazzle, the fuse can be a short. Like any parent, I have snapped at Jessica and been unfair in assessing the situation at hand. When that happened, I took great care in explaining that I was wrong to do it, asking for forgiveness, and then disciplining myself, per the house rules. It was usually a case where she wasn't paying attention to her therapy because she might be having a bad day, and because I was having a bad day, I snapped at her. My being so cross with her would make her very upset.

In those situations, I gave us both a chance to cool down, and then went to her room to tell her that it was unfair for me to snap at her because I had been upset about something that wasn't her fault. I explained that I would discipline myself by not listening to my music in my room that night so I could think about it and remember not to do that again. "I love you and I don't want to fight with you. Will you forgive me for making that mistake?" Almost always she would say it was okay, or thank me, like I thanked her, for making everything okay.

It is my belief that she saw herself and her feelings as very important, and that she felt she had some ownership in her discipline. She was never allowed to decide my punishment. But she was party to my making my list, and saw that it included things that were as important to me as the items on her list were to her. I dealt with myself firmly to set an example. I treated her with respect, always understanding that true respect is not freely given, nor to be expected. It is earned. A "do as I say and not as I do" mentality, in Jessica's case, would not provide an environment where true respect could be supported. She needed me to provide her with a "do as I do and trust what I say" model of behavior. That takes enormous commitment. It means that therapy goes on around the clock, during every waking hour. It becomes your every moment, your entire life.

Discipline is difficult for any child, but especially for children with neurological disabilities. Parents sometimes feel guilty handing down discipline. The public eye sees these parents as letting their children run loose, without repercussion, because "they don't understand what they are doing anyway." I disagree. Kids of all functioning levels need limits. Kids want limits. Kids will respect and love those who discipline them with respect and love.

That's where the 3 L's of discipline begin … with love. If you "love a lot," and you begin with love, and your motivation is that you love your child, you are less likely to have more serious difficulties later on. When your kids, Autistic or not, understand that actions designed to discipline them are motivated by your love for them, and out of parental concern, they are less likely to buck. Kids butt heads most often when they see their parents and guardians treating them unfairly, mostly because they do not fully understand the need for what is happening. Parents often say things like, "I am the parent and what I say goes. I don't have to explain to my kids why I do what I do. They know better than to talk back to me." While I understand this point of view, I know that some kids need a little more direction than that. They need to understand what is happening a little better. What works for one will not work for all. Jessica is Autistic. Her nature is one that gravitates toward needing to know what is going to happen before it happens. If she feels that she has helped to make the decisions about the activity at hand, her participation in that activity is congenial.

The second "L," laughing, is also essential to discipline. Every opportunity to laugh with your kids, about anything at all, will go a long way in helping you to be a good disciplinarian. Laughter is healing. Physical humor, such as slipping on banana peels and the like, is fine if it works. Verbal humor or jokes about things are always good, too. Get a joke book. Talk about a joke, and why it's funny. You will be doing your child a great service in showing how important humor is.

Every time I discipline Jessica, I give her an example from my own life where something similar happened to me, and tell her what I learned from it. Frequently I make fun of myself to get her to laugh, to illustrate how important it is to be able to laugh at oneself. It's sad to note how humorless some people are; far too many adults take themselves much too seriously.

Once Jessica and I have established that the discipline exists because I love her, and we have laughed out loud to lighten the mood a little, we get down to the business of the third and final "L": learning the lesson. We talk about the important points that need to be made and the behaviors that need to be changed. We restate that Jessica is a good person, that she is human and makes mistakes, and that mistakes are okay as long as you are learning from them and growing. We decide on a proper disciplinary action and how long it should last, and once we agree, we hug each other and then get back to whatever business needs attending.

I am a lucky mom, and have a remarkable teenage daughter. She and I are extremely close. Even now, we still use this system of discipline. Jessica got behind in Algebra II, and had some catch-up to do. I went to the school and met with the teacher. We agreed on a plan and exchanged email addresses so we could easily stay in touch.

This morning, I received an email telling me that Jessica had been caught doing English work in algebra class. I talked to Jessica, and told her that her teacher had sent me an email. I didn't say what the message was about, leaving that open. It could have been about a homework assignment, about her interim grades, etc. Jessica admitted to being reprimanded in class the previous day, and also admitted that it wasn't a good practice to do what she had been doing – not paying full attention in algebra. She voiced the opinion that she felt as if we were spying on her, but that it made her feel good that we cared. She said that she realized she needed to only work on algebra stuff in algebra class.

Throughout our talk, there were no raised voices, and no tears. She wore a long, serious face, but she was not angry at me. I simply expressed what was expected of her, so that the behavior would change.

If this behavior changes, it is over. However, if she steps over the line again, she will lose some privileges from her list. She knows this. Near the end of our conversation, I told her that it wasn't exactly a covert operation that her teacher and I had going, and that she shouldn't feel as if we were spying on her. As long as she was doing all the right things in class, she was flying on her own like everyone else. "Jessica," I said, "you're like a trapeze artist performing amazing feats every day, and we are just like a safety net under you. We help to identify problems so that you don't miss the next swing you have to catch!" She smiled, liking that picture in her mind. Then she exclaimed, "Ooooo … They wear a lot of sequins!" Then suddenly she screwed up her face and said "But I don't know about all that spandex!" Her list is constantly changing as she matures. The list currently consists of computer time, TV time, phone time, and video game time; Barbie left our world long ago. I sort of hated to see her go, but it was for the best. After all, with her trillion hot-pink accessories, there would be no space left in Jessica's room.

CHAPTER SIX

Making Verbal Contact

"Talk to Me — in English, Please!"

I t is hard to fathom now that my little chatterbox was once so silent. These days she and I have wonderful conversations, and she writes the most amazing stories. We also sing together, which is great fun. My bachelor's degree is in vocal music performance. I began training Jessica's voice when she was 6, and started using more advanced formal techniques at age 12 when her voice changed. Music helped to eliminate the characteristically "singsong" and "echolalic" qualities that many Autistic persons carry in their voices. But years before we started singing, we had to learn to talk to each other. We started with Barbie, as mentioned earlier.

Our Barbies lived a great life and had wonderful adventures – just ask any member of our therapy team. They took great voyages abroad; they performed in operas; they went to cooking school in Paris (they even spoke a little French!). They were true cosmopolitan Barbies. They also had a wonderful sense of humor, and they all thought that 5-year-old Jessica was a great person, and did the best they could to build her self-esteem. She would be transfixed as they talked about her during the sessions. And what child wouldn't be? It was a magnificent drama being played out in front of her; she was the star, the center of attention, but at the same time, all she could do was watch.

The dramas were short, and at the end, the therapist interacted with Jessica about what had happened in the story. She slowly began to build a vocabulary. Barbie would often have the same troubles as

Jessica. Barbie might be having trouble at school, because she bit another girl. Teresa is Barbie's friend. Teresa tells Barbie that biting is not a good way to behave, and explains why it is wrong to bite other people. Then Barbie bites Teresa and makes her cry, and Teresa tells the teacher doll. Barbie is in trouble. Jessica's face is very serious.

I am watching the session outside the door, and my face is serious, too. What I know that the therapist probably doesn't know is that Jessica thinks that the Barbie doll will bite her now. She may be afraid of the doll. I am right. Jessica is transfixed on Barbie. She is lost to the remainder of the lesson. I step in, explaining that Barbie is pretend. I show Jessica that Barbie doesn't have any teeth, and we go immediately to the questions about the lesson. It is a fairly good session. However, the only thing that Jessica remembers is that Barbie is a bad girl. Barbie bit Teresa. Bad Barbie. She makes a sad face and then hums to herself.

As I mentioned, everything in the house at that time was labeled, and we worked with *Hooked on Phonics*. In addition, I read to Jessica as much as she would allow me to. She didn't allow much contact. She didn't like to be cuddled. She would go rigid when you touched or hugged her, and didn't like to sit on the lap of any adult. She enjoyed working with *Hooked on Phonics*, but we would have to put the music on, and she would work her way around the coffee table and on and off the sofa. In the meantime, I would chase her with the cards. The English sounds that she made came out broken, stilted, almost as if they were a second language.

I kept the memory of the afternoon when she had said "bottle" ever fresh in my mind. I knew that she had a wealth of words in her head, and in her mouth. She wasn't saying them, and it was partly because I hadn't been making her say them. I had enabled her to point and grunt her way through things. I had become accustomed to her jargon, and had learned the meanings of some of her gibberish. Recordings of her sounds from that time are fascinating. They have a distinct rhythm like any language. It has a dynamic linguistic pattern, and if you could transcribe it, you could likely even punctuate it. I believe that her language truly meant something to her. That's fine, but we are English speakers in my household and I am a stubborn woman. If she had learned that language, she can learn another, I said to myself.

≡✪

I sat her in her booster seat one afternoon and I told her that I understood what she was saying, but that she was going to have to speak English. That was the new rule. She knew English, I emphasized. She understood it, and she could speak it. She made the sounds saying she was hungry.

I nodded and said. "Speak to me in English, please." Today was the day. I was standing my ground.

She made her sounds again.

I repeated, "In English, please," and went about getting her dinner.

Jessica watched me making her dinner.

I sat it on the counter. I sat at the table in front of her and told her she could have dinner. "Just ask in English." "You can do it."

We had been at it for half an hour when out it finally came.

"HUNGRY!" She screamed.

And here came immediate gratification, a plate of food to the rescue. I sat and watched her eat, wondering how many parents were losing battles with their children because they were afraid to get into the fight and didn't have the patience and persistence to see it through.

Two weeks later, she asked me for a glass of milk, brokenly, by saying "Glass of milk, please Mommy." Now try telling me she didn't know any English! For a while the language came out sounding like a second language. And for more than three years, it was the characteristic singsongy Autistic voicing. But she no longer does this. It took years of conditioning, and lots of vocal training. And she also had to deal with quite a bit of echolalia.

It was wonderful to hear her voice as she found it. She was chattering away. Before long, Barbie was talking to me about everything, and there were not enough hours in the day to discuss all the things that Barbie had to do. Her teachers at school were amazed at Jessica's sudden progress. When she found her voice, it was apparent that she had learned to read during the *Hooked on Phonics* sessions, and having everything labeled in the house helped, too, I am certain. So she had an enormous vocabulary from the start. It was music to my ears. It was an answer to prayers.

There were lots of questions initially about what I had done. I was asked to speak to parents' groups and I began telling Jessica's story. Folks began calling me, having heard that I was having success with my Autistic child. I gave talks, and I talked to whoever called me; mostly, I told people to be persistent and consistent and not to give up. In the meantime, I continued to work. There was still so much to be done!

As Jessica continued to progress, we discovered another difficulty. She couldn't control the volume level of her voice. She talked to me as if she were trying to shout over a rock guitarist tuning up at full blast. We finally devised a system, with the help of her therapists at school, to address this issue. Voice levels were given numbers from 0 to 6, with 1 being a whisper, and 6 being a shout, or an outside voice. A normal conversation voice was a level 3. When talking, I would be able to give Jessica a verbal cue, like "Jessica, you just used an outside voice, that's a number 5 voice. It's really loud. Can you try to use a number 3 voice to talk to me?" She would try again. If I needed her to be quiet, I could ask for a zero. With some practice, she could respond to the verbal cues. After years of this, she can now monitor herself without reminders and is quite used to speaking in normal conversational tones.

The child who once had so much trouble communicating is now bilingual. Her English is beautiful. In fact, she speaks English as well or better than many adults. And she is functional in Japanese. She's doing well in her French class at school. Last weekend she told me of a friend at school who is teaching her to count in Korean. Then she proceeded to rattle off numbers to 39, in Korean.

Music to my ears, still, English or not …

Jessica Speaks: On How Hooked on Phonics Worked for Me

I remember that while I was learning English, there were a lot of music tapes. I even remember my Mom using the flip cards with letters and words on them. I remember most the "k" sound, of the letter c in the word click. And I remember all the yellow sticky notes all over our house. I also remember all the silly poses my mom used to make when she would show them to me. It made me feel like laughing, but I didn't laugh a lot until I learned about my emotions. Before I learned about emotions, I might cry when I meant to laugh, and laugh when I meant to get mad. I couldn't tell the difference. I didn't know what the facial looks meant. They were just looks. It didn't mean anything.

It turned out that emotions made a lot of difference after all, not only to other people, but to me as well. When I understood emotions, I got a better view of myself. I knew what I was feeling, and I started learning what other people were feeling. It was when I learned about emotions that I got really close to my Mom, because I understood what she was feeling. That's what still keeps us close.

Because I understand now, I will never have to be alone. I will never have to be in "The Void" again. Ever.

CHAPTER SEVEN

Making Eye Contact

"Don't Look at Me in That Tone of Voice, Young Lady!"

Ahhh ... the focus factor. Many individuals on the Autism Spectrum don't make eye contact, or make eye contact only for a brief moment, before looking away. It's too difficult for them to sustain this common nonverbal communication gesture. For many Spectrum kids, the visual stimulation involved in maintaining eye contact is so intense that they find it almost painful. At the very least, it is so distracting that they have to look away and focus the eyes somewhere else in order to be able listen to conversational speech and process it effectively. For this reason, many individuals on the Spectrum are misunderstood as being "aloof," or as not listening.

Eye contact, at least for a first impression when people meet one another, is important in our society, and helps people to read facial cues more accurately. I wanted to address this in our therapy sessions because Jessica would not look at me at all.

I knew from the beginning that this fight would be one of the big ones. I also knew that this would be one of the more important battles to win. I chose this fight because lack of eye contact is one of the most "identifying" behaviors of the Spectrum. We are perfectly happy on the spectrum. We are not looking for a "cure." However, there are ways to handle identifying behaviors and make life easier to manage, first and foremost for the individual on the Spectrum. I chose to teach Jessica to make eye contact so that first as an adolescent, when she was able to advocate for herself, people would listen to her and take her seriously. And later as an adult when applying for a job, for example, she would be seen as the intelligent, talented person that she is.

The world needs to see "person," "talented," "confident" and "intelligent" as much as possible. If Jessica were unable to make eye contact, all the world would ever see in a first impression of her would be a "disability." People would see a "disorder" instead of the bright and beautiful person that she is. Giving her every available advantage is my job. Failing to try to give her all the reasons why others see the need to make eye contact, and to try to re-train her to do so, would have been a disservice to her. She wanted to be polite, and enjoys using good manners.

Eventually, we added eye contact to the list of manners. But she needed the ability to focus her eyes on more than just people's faces. It was a fight, and she won more than the ability to look the world in the face. Focusing her attention with both eyes, and holding her attention became an "invitation" of sorts, out of her own lonely world and into the light. When Jessica accepted my invitations to come out of The Void by focusing on items placed in her twisting hand, she looked at them with both eyes instead of out of the corners, and I knew that I had her full attention. Those moments were sacred.

When loud sounds occurred in the house, Jessica's eyes would go immediately to the area the sounds were coming from. They might not stay there for long, but they would travel there. She had become, by about age 4, very adept at using her peripheral range. She could build towers of blocks on the floor without actually looking at the blocks. She could simply choose a block and drop it to the side, and it would stack neatly atop the one she had just placed. While these feats of miniature architecture were spellbinding to watch, they were nonetheless not efficient. Besides, as fascinating as a "gift" like this appears, it has little value to her in the real world. It seemed to me that her time would be better spent not on honing the peripheral range, but focusing on "focusing" instead.

I talked to Jessica a great deal about how I wanted her to look at me. She would not look at me. I knew that the "Look at Me" campaign was going to be a tough challenge. I sat with Jessica at the table in the kitchen, as I had done so many times before, when I launched into it.

"Jessica, we have some work to do together."

She fidgets, kicks the bottom of the table and squeals.

"Jessica, listen. We have to work on something. We have to look at each other. We are going to look at each other and count. I think we should do it in the living room, okay? Are you listening to me?"

Jessica bangs her hands on the top of the high chair and shakes her head back and forth. Finally she leans to the side. She appears to be looking at the ceiling, but she is looking at me out of the side of her eye. I start again.

"Jessica. You must learn to look at me with both eyes. We will go into the living room, and you and I will look at each other and then count together. You might not like it, but it will be a new game. Trust Mommy. I will not hurt you, okay? We have to do it and we will have some fun. I love you so much. We will sit and I will hold your head, and when you look at me, I will let go, and then we will count together. If we count high, that's good, okay?"

She is still, watching me, and rubbing the top of the high chair.

"So. I will sit with you, and I will hold your head, and you look at me, and we count 'one, two, three, four … like that, okay? We will have a snack first. Then we will play a game and then have another snack. Okay, Jessica?"

We sat on the floor facing each other, and I braced her legs and hips with mine. Immediately, she went rigid. Then I took her face in my hands and brought it close to mine, waiting for her to look at my eyes. I kept talking to her, telling her that when she looked at my eyes, I would let go.

The first time, this did not go smoothly. She kicked and bucked, and hit me in the face. She butted me in the face with her head, screaming at the top of her lungs throughout. This continued for several minutes, but then she made eye contact. As promised, I let go and started counting. She stopped screaming when I started counting, as if something in her memory had clicked on something I had said. Then she looked away. Clamp! My hands came down again on the sides of her head and brought her face back to mine, and we started again. Square one.

Eye contact. I let go. One, two, three. She looks away. CLAMP. Buck and scream. Eye contact. I let go. One, two, three, four. She looks away. CLAMP. Buck and scream. Eye contact. I let go. One, two, three, four, five, six. She looks away. CLAMP. Buck and scream. She slaps me in the face. Lots of tears. We are both exhausted.

After an hour, I have a swollen lip and can taste blood in my mouth. Jessica is sobbing. I say, "Look at me." She screams "NO!" and cries. "Okay, then tomorrow," I say.

We continue like this every day for weeks. Eventually, we begin to count together. We got into the twenties, and the thirties. Then into the forties. There were still outbursts but they were lighter than before. Jessica still got upset at times, and occasionally she would still hit me in the face when she got very tired.

In the meantime, her therapists at school remarked that Jessica was making excellent progress – she was paying better attention than ever before. We kept working. I introduced the verbal cues into everyday speech with things like, "Look at me when you talk to me, please," and "In my eyes, please." As time went on, she showed more and more progress. In some cases, when I simply pointed to my face, the motion of my hand would remind her to make eye contact.

It was an ongoing battle, but we seemed to be making headway. She would look at me from time to time and smile a forced smile. Her smiles almost never reached all the way to her eyes, however.

As she has matured, through puberty and into high school, we have discussed several times the need for making eye contact. She understands that on many occasions, you get one opportunity to make an impression on somebody. Within minutes of meeting a new person, he or she has usually sized you up and formed an opinion – if you are honest or dishonest, if you are nice or not nice; and if they should trust you or not. People trust you more if you look at them in their eyes. It makes people feel better.

I knew that if I could teach her to master this little social trick, it would be a great service to her. Better still, if she were able to make eye contact without causing herself any physical discomfort, it would be giving her the gift of being able to read an enormous amount of social cues from the faces of people around her – and of her instructors, of her peers, and her parents as well!

Many people are instantly uneasy when a person does not look them in the eyes. Jessica and I agree that sometimes putting somebody else at ease is important. Being able to make eye contact can make a huge difference in how the world will treat her. If she can do it, it's one less thing that might trip her up and keep her from getting everything in life that she wants. When that's the motivation for going on with therapy, who can argue that Jessica keeps working to better herself all the time?

As part of working on learning to make and sustain eye contact, we spent countless hours with magazines, as she memorized different emotions on faces. I taught her to look into the eyes, and to dance between the eyes instead of blankly staring as often happens when individuals on the spectrum learn to make eye contact.

Almost immediately, Jessica began to recognize faces. Before, she only knew the people on the therapy team, but just three months from the time we began the "Look at Me" therapy, suddenly she was able to tell me about people at the bank, or at the college where I worked. It was thrilling. It was unbelievable progress. We had all previously been little more than shadows in her life. Once in a while, I could see a light behind her eyes when she smiled. It was enough for me to keep pushing.

Today, Jessica has no trouble making eye contact, and has an easy, contagious grin. As in so many of the other battles, simple conditioning worked in bringing about this change. It is remarkable how important eye contact is in our society. I am relieved that we were able to address this with Jessica, thereby alleviating the social stigma associated with a wandering stare. The biggest relief, for both of us, was yet to come.

Jessica Speaks:
On Making Eye Contact

Although I normally remember what happened when I was younger, I can't seem to remember anything about the eye contact sessions except for one thing. I remember feeling tired during a session. I wanted to stop because I was close to Mom's face. Sometimes I feel like I am in my own personal bubble and that if people get too close, they might pop it. I felt that the only way to stop Mom from getting me close to her face was by hitting her. Maybe if I hit her, she would stop. But she didn't stop. I would try again and again. But she would never stop. So I gave up.

Not having eye contact is another way of being in "The Void." People think you aren't listening, or aren't honest, or aren't friendly. Therefore, they don't take much interest in you. What's sad is that this is another stereotype, and this annoys me. Even though I didn't have eye contact, I was a good listener. I was called stupid and inconsiderate anyway.

I'm not having all the problems I used to have any more. A major part of that, I know, is because I can look at people in their eyes. It's a lot easier to tell what other people are thinking or feeling, which is sometimes difficult for me. If I look at them, I can also tell if they are listening to me, and if they are interested or bored. I am better now that I can do this. It's a lot better than staring into The Void.

CHAPTER EIGHT

Making Human Contact

"You're Going to Hug Me No Matter What!"

It's not that Jessica wouldn't give you a hug. It's that she didn't process touch very well. She didn't like to be touched. She didn't like being picked up. She didn't want to be hugged or cuddled. She didn't want to hold your hand. It drove me bananas. It's heartbreaking for parents. And you can imagine my dismay when she wouldn't allow my parents to smother her with kisses and hugs. Everyone wanted to love her, she was such a pretty little girl. Little blonde head and blue eyes, and always dressed up really cute, thanks to my mother. Everything about Jessica just called out for a hug, but when you got close, she would go rigid and push you away.

I watched her constantly, looking for an opportunity. I would snatch a hug from behind, quickly, and she gradually got accustomed to this. I would also steal kisses, but those usually made her mad, so I tried to keep that to a minimum. I did kiss her forehead when she slept. In fact, I often went into her room and stroked her hair and kissed her when she was sleeping. Sometimes I would pick her up and hold her for a while. It was wonderful to just be able to hold her.

Using behavior modification, we were fighting a war on many fronts: personal hygiene, reading, language, eye contact, social interaction, Jessica's many self-stimulatory tics, her explosive behavioral episodes. And, as illustrated, we were doing all this while keeping track of our times on a matrix so as not to be a slave to any sort of pattern or schedule, consistent with chaos theory.

In all the reading that I had been doing about behavioral development, I have found studies about touch and the importance of touch to the healthy development of the human psyche. I was constantly thinking about the days before Jessica regressed. She had been very affectionate. She and I held hands. She'd loved to give kisses. She wanted me to hold her all the time. I had a hunch that she still craved this kind of physical affection, but that Autism had affected her ability to process it, making her confused and frustrated. If conditioning could bring about such tremendous improvements in other parts of her life, why not here?

I knew before I began that I would be the primary facilitator of this part of the therapy, at least in the beginning, because I was the only one whom Jessica trusted enough to touch her. I decided that bedtime would be the best time to start. This was because I needed some leverage. I needed a trigger. Jessica wanted me to sing to her at night. She usually requested the songs and I sang. As part of this therapy, I explained to her that I would only sing if she would allow me to rub her hand as I sang. At first she resisted, and when she pulled her hand away, I stopped singing. She learned quickly that to get me to keep singing, she would have to remain still. I rubbed her hand lightly as I sang. The next night I moved on to the wrist. Each day I would move a little further. As I moved to areas that were more sensitive, I explained to her that I was getting her used to being touched. Some nights, she would whine. There were also tears a few nights, but she became used to being touched, even on the backs of her knees, the bottoms of her feet, and the nape of her neck. It was only a couple of months before she was able to request a song, and then turn over and let me rub her back as I sang. Usually, she would go to sleep before I finished.

To condition her further, we moved to textiles and other surfaces. We used every sort of fabric swatch I could find. Velvet, silk, satin, burlap, cotton, nylon, rayon, and denim. Then came blocks of wood, sandpaper, metal, chains, stones, shells, beads, sequins, plastic, aluminum foil, rubber, foam, hairbrushes – anything I could think of that would stimulate her sensitive nerve endings, anything that might fire her up. We took them one at a time, one each night or for however many nights were necessary until she could tolerate them. For instance, she needed three nights for plastic, and hairbrushes took a couple of weeks, but by the end, she had no significant reaction to anything. I was confident then that the major conditioning work had been done. After that time, I no longer had to worry about what kind of clothes to get for her. She didn't fuss with appliqués on her clothes, or with lace, collars or buttons that bothered her.

In her kindergarten year, when she was 5 years old, Jessica was beginning to open up. After I would sing her songs at night, I would kiss her goodnight. I had noticed that she had stopped wiping the kisses away. One night, when I was in a bit of a rush to get her to bed because I had a paper to write for a class, I sang her songs quickly and got back to work, only to hear her whining for me a few minutes later. When I went in to check on her, I found her crying. I asked her what was wrong. She said that I hadn't kissed her. In my rush I had forgotten! I kissed her little cheeks a dozen times, crying myself. I had been right about her need for physical affection!

As a parent of a child with Autism, it would have been easy to assume that she wanted the comfort of the routine, that the crying was the result of that need; however, that night was a breakthrough night for her. She wanted to give ME a kiss. She put her little arms around my neck and kissed my cheek. That expression made her so happy. Her face was literally glowing. I told her that she made me such a happy Mommy. I saw her smile reach all the way to her eyes that night.

I am happy that I discovered that Jessica needed to be touched, and wanted that kind of affection. However, it's a double-edged sword. She wanted to hug everyone after she got used to it. She would hug the other kids at school, their parents, the janitor, and strangers at the mall. I had to be so careful, so watchful at all times. She became a very loving child. It was a wonderful transformation. Eventually we had to talk to her about the fact that other people don't like to hug quite as much as she does. That was a little baffling to Jessica.

We had a lot of catching up to do. She sat in my lap as much as possible. She and I held hands a lot, even when most of the other kids her age didn't think it was "cool." It was nice to have some human contact back. She had been gone a long time. It is easy to see that it was part of her life that she had been missing.

She is still the greatest hugger.

Jessica Speaks:
On Becoming a Butterfly

I had a dream one night in Japan. In my dream it seemed so real. It was about what my life would have been like without my Mom. I noticed that I kept looking into space, or looking down. I was violent when anyone touched me. Sometimes I was quiet; sometimes I threw chairs; and sometimes I screamed at the top of my lungs and kicked and hit people. The dream went on. Nobody could talk to me, and I couldn't talk to anyone. There was truly a sense of loneliness. I wanted to stop this madness, but it was like I was invisible. There was nothing I could do.

I woke up the next morning and realized that it was just a dream. I felt a feeling of thankfulness. I got up and had my normal morning, and Mom offered to fix my hair for me. I didn't tell her about the dream, but I told her about my thankfulness as best as I could.

"Mom," I said, "about the Autism thing …"

"Yes. What is it?" She said.

"Thank you for not stopping."

There was a glimmer in her eyes like she was about to cry. She didn't say anything. She hugged me. It was a big hug. I felt like crying, too – the happy kind of crying, because you know you are loved.

Mom says I am becoming a butterfly. Like a caterpillar, I was born warm and fuzzy, and then I went into a dark place. Now I am emerging from that dark place. Because of my work with Mom, I can fly solo, and free.

CHAPTER NINE

Making Dinner

"Yes, You're Going to Eat That"

J essica has a healthy appetite. I talk to many parents of children on the Autism Spectrum who complain that it is difficult to get them to eat balanced meals because they will only eat certain foods. My stepson Averie also has Autism. I have been in Averie's life for a little more than two years now and I am still working on the food angle with him. It is a difficult battle with many people on the Autism Spectrum.

For many persons on the spectrum, the mealtime routine might consist of eating at exactly the same time, every day without fail, always with the same person or persons. This is what I call the food repertoire. Further, the foods must generally be what is expected. They must be foods that they are familiar with, and prepared in the way that they are accustomed to. They may eat in exactly the same fashion every time, or eat every French fry first and then eat the hamburger. Sometimes the foods mustn't touch, or they must be all one color, or a certain brand. Due to these restrictions, the thought of leaving the safety of home to go to a restaurant is terrifying to some.

With Jessica, like so many of her behaviors, I had to make her eating habits part of the house rules. She understood house rules. The rules were that she had to eat what we were having for dinner. True to chaotic form, we never ate at the same time. We had 30 different dinner times every month.

She also was required to eat many different foods. She would get something that was her favorite, but only after she had tried something that wasn't a favorite food. It would be served like a course. She could eat a new food while waiting for me to finish setting the table perhaps. She grew to love green vegetables this way. If she was turning up her nose at something, I made note of it, and prepared it differently to see if she would like it another way.

It wasn't easy to train her to eat whatever I handed to her. At first my attempts were met with a lot of resistance. Kids like what they like. Hot dogs or bologna, French fries, pizza, Jello, ice cream, chicken noodle soup, ramen noodles, cereal, macaroni and cheese, peanut butter sandwiches, chicken nuggets and waffle sticks: Sadly, all of it processed and full of preservatives and pre-packaged. They know what to expect. They get to know the colors of the packaging so you have to get the same brands every time. And you have to prepare it the same way every time. We mothers agonize, reading the labels, wanting to give them a little better nutrition and aching to get a piece of fruit inside our kids every once in a while.

I told Jessica that she would be allowed to have one of her favorites, but only after she ate what I gave her to eat. If she didn't eat what we were having, she wouldn't be eating until the next meal. That was the rule.

She called my bluff only once. The first time, when she didn't like the look of my beef stew, she said a series of "no no no no"s while the rest of us ate. I stood my ground; was firm about the rules. She had eaten breakfast. She would have a snack two or three hours later, so I wasn't worried that she would starve. I was making a point with her that was of great importance.

Jessica obviously didn't think I was serious. This was a battle of wills in a sense. A "Will Mom give me something else to eat if I refuse to eat what she's given me?" My answer was "No, you will eat this or you will wait until the next meal because you will learn to eat what's served." She refused to eat the stew. I took it away, asked her to leave the table, and told her we'd eat at snack time. She motioned for a hotdog. I told her we were having stew. She eventually gave up and went to her room. She had her snack a while later, and ate a huge dinner that night. She didn't turn her nose up at anything – including vegetables. She ate everything in front of her.

I didn't behave angrily. I was just firm. Those were the rules, and Jessica had to abide by them. I never yell and scream. I state the rules.

With children on the Spectrum, initiating a system of house rules is fairly simple. It's being firm about the rules that takes an extraordinary high level of commitment.

When Jessica learned that trying new foods wasn't going to kill her, I began to use her "bravery" as an opportunity to build her self-esteem. I would praise her efforts in front of the team members, who would act impressed that she was trying new foods. She soon gained respect for all sorts of new experiences. I was able to take her to live in Japan, where we ate a diet quite different from one to which most Americans are accustomed. Not only did she survive; she thrived. Today, Jessica will approach a table laden with foods she has never seen, and inquire about them instead of backing away. Nevertheless, it's likely that she'll tilt her head to the side and purse her lips thoughtfully, before digging right in.

I don't insist that you have to clean your plate before you get up from the table. I have come to the realization that kids don't need to be stuffed to the gills, as long as they eat a balanced diet. However, I see the benefit in the ability to try new foods and enjoy them. It opens up a whole new social realm. Those persons who refuse to take part limit themselves tremendously. My rule for Jessica was along the lines of "you don't have to like it, but you do have to try it."

When I tell people about our system of introducing new foods, and that Jessica was required to eat it before she was allowed to eat her favorite food, many immediately think of my poor daughter choking down a huge bowl of brussel sprouts while I waved a hotdog in front of her face. Yes, I made her try sprouts. The operative word here is "try." She ate one brussel sprout while I spread peanut butter on a sandwich. It so happens that she didn't mind it too much. It wasn't her favorite vegetable. It's not mine either. But she tried it, and we eat it on occasion.

It wasn't unusual for me to open a can of green beans and give her a few to eat on her tray while I prepared the rest of her dinner. Green beans are still her favorite veggie. Occasionally, I would substitute carrots, broccoli, or celery. Then I went for broke, and threw yellow squash and zucchini in the mix. Before long, she would eat about anything I handed her. It took getting through to her that she would be playing by my rules.

This sounds oversimplified. I am not claiming that it was easy. At the beginning, none of it is easy. It is as if you are standing at the base of a mountain deciding whether to climb or to camp. If your purpose for the trip was to reach the summit, you are stopping short of your goal if you are not prepared to meet the challenges the climb will bring. It will be a little rocky, but that's part of the challenge.

If you are unprepared to be firm with your children when they protest, you are stopping short of another goal: Encouraging them to expand their horizons. So you don't like broccoli yourself. Fine. Will you not serve it to your child because you don't like it? Will you not encourage him to eat it? It's healthy. It's also a healthy attitude to adopt towards new things in general. Change starts out as a very small thing. The journey up that mountain starts by taking those first few steps on the hiking path.

I have talked to a lot of parents about their children's food repertoires. In many cases, these folks travel around with peanut butter crackers and cans of Vienna sausages and Skittles in their bags, because there is nothing that their kids want to eat in any restaurant. Many children are on special diets, such as gluten-free or casein-free, which is a different matter altogether. But by and large, many spectrum kids pick up certain food habits in childhood that are hard to break. In some cases, I have discovered that the parents concede to their kid, because it is easier to buy a certain brand of food and have it on hand than to engage in battle over it, re-train the child's palate, and give the child freedom to choose anything from the menu, anywhere in the world.

Such unhealthy eating choices could lead some of these kids down the road to health problems like diabetes or obesity. Besides, they miss a lot of great stuff. I know one child on the spectrum who refuses to eat any brown food. His reasoning is that dirt is brown, so all brown food must be made of dirt. This means, of course, that he will never even TRY chocolate, for example. Imagine a life without chocolate.

Without my insistence that Jessica try new things, she would probably never have tried anything outside her favorite foods. As an adult, she might still be living a severely unhealthy life on a diet of overly processed, sodium-rich foods. Similarly, without my insistence that Jessica try listening to all sorts of music, she likely would not have dis-covered the artists who ultimately inspired her to compose her own music. Without my insistence that she try to open her mind to new ways of thinking about things, she likely would never have discovered that she was able to think critically on her own. She gained confidence.

It's useful for parents to pick an example that their child can relate to easily to help to establish the trust base. Food is easy. Kids relate to that. Setting up a new rule about trying new things is a good place to start. But be prepared to back it up. You must be prepared to do yourself what you ask your child to do. Respect is earned; it is not given out for free. To illustrate, take what I call "the bell pepper incident."

I don't like bell peppers. I have tried them, and I don't like them. I had successfully introduced a lot of vegetables into Jessica's diet, even ones that I liked only marginally, like boiled okra. I was very proud of the efforts that I had made. One night we went to eat at a friend's house. It was wonderful to be able to say we could attend the dinner party, because a couple of years prior to that we wouldn't have been able to go at all.

My friend, a wonderful person, asked me if there were any special restrictions. With obvious pride in my voice, I answered that she could prepare anything she wished. I think she made the bell peppers to test Jessica. She didn't know that it would be a test for me as well. My own words would float back at me, and I would be forced to either eat them, or worse – eat an entire bell pepper.

When we were served, I'm sure I had an obvious look of horror on my face. I wasn't digging right in as I typically do. Jessica asked her usual questions about what was being served. I answered as best I could about the ingredients. Suddenly she stopped and asked me why I wasn't eating. I am usually honest with her. A lot of parents would play the role of "eat it, yum yum yum, it's gooooood" and play it off so that it's not a big deal. I was lucky that I was among friends who thought that it was funny that I didn't like peppers. There was another entrée, so my friend wasn't hurt by my admission to Jessica.

I am honest about stuff like this with Jessica. I told her that peppers weren't something that I liked all that much. I took a long sniff and said that it smelled delicious, though. Without hesitation, my own words came back at me in her innocent but convincing tone. "You don't have to like it, Mommy. But you do need to try it." Then, without batting an eyelash, she put her napkin in her lap, and dug right in. She was 8 years old.

And I ate the whole pepper! It wasn't the most enjoyable dish I ever ate, but it was nutritious and filling. When we were finished with dinner, Jessica patted my hand and said that she was proud of how brave I was for trying something new. My friends and I laughed. I told my friend that I was happy she'd made the peppers. The incident had shown that Jessica could apply the techniques she had learned. I was able to use that example many times in future discussions with her.

You have to be prepared to do whatever you ask your child to do. It's the same principle as the manager who refuses to work the fax machine, or the officer who refuses to go into the fight – if you're going to have your child eat broccoli, then bon appetite to you, too!

Once they have expanded their horizon, have learned what they like and don't like, and can trust you to be honest about it, and to be brave alongside them, you and your children are home free. You can agree on a well-balanced diet you both like and then stick to that. Just be careful not to let that routine be the ruler of the house. Our world is more chaotic than that, so we'd better prepare our children to deal with that.

If you allow your child to only eat what I call "the current food repertoire" and never branch out and try new things, you are doing both your child and yourself a great disservice. You may have to travel with peanut butter crackers forever, and always make explanations to friends, relatives, and fellow diners at restaurants. However, you may be able to remedy some of the problem by being proactive about food, and being willing to take on the fight.

I took Jessica to Japan when she was 9 years old. For two years, we ate everything they gave us. And, there were plenty of opportunities for Jessica to turn up her nose at what was being served. We love Japanese food, but authentic Japanese food and what is served here, or Americanized Japanese food, are two completely different things. At some points, especially because of the language barrier, we were unable to identify what we were eating. I will admit that there were a few cases when that was probably a good thing. Jessica ate with abandon. She was trained to try everything, and knew how to handle things that she determined she didn't like after she'd tried them.

At the beginning, and in keeping with the regimen, I wrote down what Jessica was served at mealtimes and made certain that we never had the same combinations over and over again. It's too easy for pattern to re-form. In this way, it became easy for 5-year-old Jessica not only to try one kind of food after another but to transition from one daily activity to another, like the rest of us do. It made life easier for both of us. For example, if I received a phone call in the afternoon from a friend in town for the day, inviting me to dinner, I would be able to enjoy my evening out because I could call a sitter for Jessica, or she might be able to attend with me. I was also able to drop by the grocery store and pick up items as needed, without making special trips. Some individuals with Autism cannot do this; it is a violation of their routine.

Jessica has several adult friends. Granted, they began as my friends. However, she keeps them by her own merit, because they like her and she is an interesting young person. She is also a budding artist. An artist friend of ours recently invited her to stay for an overnight visit, so off she went, like a little jetsetter. Because of the efforts that Jessica and I have made together towards eliminating her rigid routines, she is able to take advantage of opportunities like this, as any kid her age could.

And that's what it's all been about from the beginning. It has not been about providing her as many opportunities at as normal a life as she can possibly have. That's really the wrong way to think about it. It has been about improving the quality of the life that she has to its fullest. And if that includes bell peppers, then so be it.

Jessica Speaks: On Trying New Stuff

I love food. I think I get what people mean when they talk about "comfort food." Food makes you happy. The more new foods I try, the more things I find that I like. What started out as nine foods turned into dozens, and then dozens turned into hundreds. I can't exactly explain what it's like, but it's like a feeling of achievement. It's like climbing over an obstacle, or riding a scary ride in an amusement park. If you don't like the ride, you don't have to ride it again. The same goes for what you eat. If you don't like the way it tastes, you don't have to eat it again. But you do have to try it, or you might miss a grand opportunity!

Because I can eat anything, I blend in really easy. I don't stick out in the crowd, as someone picky or self-conscious about the things that I eat. Most people that you meet aren't like that. They know what they like and don't like, just like me!

It might sound funny, but it helped me to know more about myself. It helped me to gain some confidence in myself. I'm not afraid to try new things in general. Not just food, but other things, too – like rides at amusement parks, and horror movies, and different music styles.

I am able to go anywhere and do anything. When we lived in Japan, my mom told me one day that she was going to teach me how to snorkel. I was a bit afraid of the mask, and that my nose would get clogged up or that I wouldn't be able to breathe through that tube thingy. Then my mom went through the whole story of how I need to try new things, just like I tried new foods, and that I could overcome my fear of new experiences.

She was right. There were so many fish and unique types of coral that I could see under the water. The beauty of the bluish-green water was outstanding. I never realized that it was really that color under there! The light shining over the water made it seem like white crystals were floating all around me, and it was an experience that will never leave me.

I suppose the moral of my story could be: Eat your broccoli and go snorkeling. Just go for it!

CHAPTER TEN

Going Into Public Again

"Life Lessons, Danger and Good Ol' Common Sense"

One of the hardest things to teach your kids – Autistic or not – is to use their heads. Some parents of teenagers may wonder how anyone ever grows into adulthood at all, given the crazy things that some kids do. The best thing that we as parents can do is to teach our children the basics of right and wrong, and then hope that they will apply that knowledge when they walk out the door and into the world.

With a child with Autism Spectrum Disorders, you have the added challenge that he may not understand that something might be dangerous. He may not be able to distinguish between fantasy and reality. He will probably have a clear understanding of the rules, but he may not understand that the rules apply to him along with everyone else. And, basic life lessons, such as the need to share or that taking candy from a store is stealing, may be completely lost on him.

Life lessons are the toughest for children on the Autism Spectrum to learn, and at the same time, they appear every day, in every teachable moment. Most kids learn the lesson that stealing is wrong when they take some candy from the store, and Mom or Dad takes them back to the store and makes the store manager reprimand them, and then make them pay for the candy. The discipline that occurs later at home is different at everyone's house.

With kids on the Autism Spectrum, there are lots of tough lessons to learn, such as how you can't buy your friends. Jessica gave all her allowance money to kids at school during her lunch period, because they told her that they would be her friends if she would pay them. This seemed reasonable to her. They also told her not to tell her parents. They let her sit at their table, but they didn't do much more than "share" her lunch, and take her money. She was never invited to any birthday parties, for example. I caught on, and stopped that little scandal. Now, Jessica can see those people coming.

Averie, at age 5, trapped in his own world, felt so much comfort from the Disney movie *Aladdin* that he thought that he was the only person in the world who owned the movie. He could not comprehend that anyone else had a copy of it. If the movie was shown at his daycare, he would have a meltdown, or would become angry if it was being played and he was not in the room. He often hid the movie in his bag, and "stole" it from the daycare even though he had two copies of the movie at home.

Life lessons don't ever stop for any of us, whether we are on the Autism Spectrum or not. Even these days, my children still need clarification of language, because they tend to take things very literally. My husband, laughing at a joke last year, said "That kills me!" In response, Averie expressed concern that Steve was going to die. These plays on words are part of our everyday therapy. This is all life lesson therapy.

I want to address life lessons first, because the mind is the computer of the body, and a life lesson is like a program for that computer. When you have finished dinner in the evening, you know that the dishes must be cleaned up. This program has already been installed in your system, hasn't it? The dishes will not clean themselves. Parents have said this to kids for generations. This is how the programs get installed. When you break down any task or chore, it can be examined with a simple "if-then" statement. Anyone who has kids, or has taken the old basic computer courses, knows what I am talking about: an "if-then" statement is a simple declarative. You have a cause and an effect, or a situation and a solution. IF "a" is present, THEN you perform "b," for the computer people. For the rest of us, it goes like this: IF you have a mess, THEN you clean it up.

Most people go from a mess to cleanup rather quickly. However, the Autistic mind often has to make stops along the way to process the information. When teaching Jessica about how to handle situations at home, I started trying to break her cycle of thinking. For example, she had a favorite cup and bowl that she liked to use. If this cup was already dirty, she would be irritated, and often insisted that it be washed right away so that she could use it to drink. If she was drinking milk during dinner and wanted juice an hour after dinner, the cup would have to be washed. I soon realized that if this cup became cracked, broken, or lost, we might find ourselves in a bad situation. Therefore, I began to introduce her to different cups, and eventually hid the favorite cup. She did not like this at first, but she gradually learned that it did not matter. I would say things like, "Use a cup like mine!" or "If you would like a drink, try this juice box …" Little by little, we got away from the cup.

One of the main tenets of any therapy lesson that I have stressed with my kids is the need to be flexible. Flexibility is so important in life. After Hurricane Fran hit North Carolina and we were without power for a while, Jessica and I walked around our devastated neighborhood and looked at the old oak trees that were blown down during the storm. Several downed trees were a hundred and fifty years old or older. When Sherman marched to the sea and burned the South during the Civil War, he marched down that street, and those trees were silent witnesses. Now, they lay splintered on the road. It was sad. But next to them, and I will never forget the lesson that they taught me, were smaller trees that had survived the onslaught. They had been flexible. They had been able to whip around in the wind, and were not ripped out of the ground. They were "bendy." I took Jessica to the base of the biggest splintered oak tree and explained to her about the importance of flexibility. I told her that success in life was learning how to be "bendy" when the winds blew hard. After all, she was only 6 years old. She wasn't too keen on big words like "flexibility." I taught that big word to her, but she glazed over. She got "bendy." Keep it on the level of the child, and you will reach her.

Wanting to use the same cup, or to drink the same kind of juice every time, or to drink juice at the same time every single day, may seem like a good idea, but there are several levels of inflexibility here. In this example, I would point out to Jessica that drinking juice is healthy. I would also agree that having favorites, like a favorite cup, is okay. I, too, have a favorite coffee cup. We would talk about that. But it should be okay to visit other people's homes and drink out of their cups. It should be okay to drink out of cups at restaurants, too. Maybe we could even drink out of a cup at Grandma's! All those cups aren't the exact same as the favorite cup, but they still work, and they are okay. At the very least, the other cups should be tried out. It means that we are brave to try new things!

Further, by trying a different kind of juice, we might find new things that we like. We could try them together! Sometimes, I would offer an incentive for trying new things, such as going to a favorite place or playing a favorite game, or trying new things. We have done combinations of all these. Finally, trying new things should be viewed as a great accomplishment. For example, when Jessica tried broccoli for the first time, I called friends on the telephone and told them all about it, triumphantly, as if she had just won an Academy Award. She was proud of herself, and was eager to try more new things.

I found that the fundamental problems with most applied behavior analysis programs were that they enabled my daughter to become comfortable with her cycle of thinking. They did not encourage her to think outside the box. They did not raise the bar. They did not expect anything besides rocking and spinning from her. Again, don't misunderstand me. It was fine with me for her to be who she was. But I thought that the whole idea was to give her the world outside that therapy room. To do so, I had to prepare her adequately for that world.

I always thought that her ways of thinking about things were fine. They still are fine. And her tastes are fine. But like everyone, she needed exposure to new things so that there were fewer surprises. It's social conditioning. At the fundamental level of social conditioning is the "if-then" statement. If somebody says "this," then you say "that," and so on. If, for example, you are out with friends, and the driver of your car is drinking alcohol, and you need a ride home, then you call a taxi. If you are arrested, then you call a lawyer. If you meet the queen, then you curtsy. It works in nearly every case.

So we started with "if" and "then." It is important to first get the child's attention. You must keep that attention at all costs. You must be prepared to start the lesson whenever you have that attention. With Jessica, I knew that I had to illustrate using big movements to keep her focusing on me. We were in the kitchen, and I will never forget about learning the meaning of "if you have a mess, then you clean it up." She was 5 years old.

I am washing the dishes, "Jessica, honey, come bring me your dishes."

She doesn't move. "Dishes dishes dishes dishes dishes …" She sings.

I stop washing. "Jessica. Dishes. To the sink. Right now. Go."

She goes, still singing. I have her attention.

"Hey," I say. "Look at this." I hold up an egg. "What would happen if I drop this egg?"

"Drop this egg." She says.

"I want to teach you about the word 'if.'"

"if if if if if if …" she sings.

"Yes, if. What would happen if I drop this egg? Pay attention."

"You will drop it."

"And then what?" I ask.

She thinks about that. "It will go down."

"Yes. And then what?" I ask.

She thinks further. "It will touch the ground."

"That's right. And then what would happen?" I ask.

She hums. I wait. She fidgets. I wait. I finally realize that she doesn't have a clue what would happen.

I push a little. "It's okay. Guess if you don't know." I urge.

"Roll to the table?" She guesses.

I stand up and hold the egg over my head and let go. It crashes to the linoleum and makes a satisfying splat at my feet. Jessica jumps, and her eyes go wide. She can't believe I have made such a mess.

"What happened to the egg, Jessica?" I ask.

"Big mess. Big mess. Mess mess mess," says Jessica.

"Yes. Big mess. What happened, though? Did it roll to the table?" I ask.

"It broke. The egg broke. Broke broke broke broke broke …," she sings. Jessica looks at the egg on the floor and back to me.

"Yep. So if you drop an egg then what?" I ask.

"It will go down," Jessica says.

Jessica is like many persons on the Spectrum who think in a very specific order. She thinks from A to B to C to D to E. The egg is released, it goes down, it touches the floor, it cracks open, and finally, there's a mess. The rest of us go immediately from A to E in our thinking. We feel that eggshell leave our fingers and start reaching for the paper towels. We've probably already seen the mess in our heads before the egg has hit the floor. I realized later that if I had dropped a hard-boiled egg, and it had bounced, she would have been baffled by that, or if I had reached and caught the egg before it hit the floor, it would have created a loop in her thinking pattern.

Incidentally, I went back to this same exercise and did both these things with her later, in teaching lessons on flexibility. I also did something similar with plastic Easter eggs and hid different treats inside to teach a lesson about surprises. But that first night, I was dealing with learning "if" and "then," and specifically, trying to get her to skip steps in her thinking pattern. It's the "work smarter, not harder" adage. I told her to cut out all the extra steps and tell me what would probably happen if I dropped that egg. It took half a dozen eggs, an entire roll of paper towels – and a lot of patience – but at the end of the session, I got the following from Jessica.

"Jessica, what happens if you drop an egg in the kitchen?"

"If you drop an egg, then it will break," she answered.

"And if you have a mess, what should you do?" I asked.

"If you have a mess, then you have to clean it up," she answered.

Applying that concept to everything else wasn't nearly as hard as you might imagine. Once Jessica had the basics of "if" and "then," she was on her way. It's the fundamental principle to everything else. All I had to do was teach her how to curtsy properly, and she was ready to meet the queen!

Distinguishing between fantasy and reality is often difficult for individuals on the Spectrum as well. Many of the persons on the Spectrum with whom I have worked describe the characters in stories with such detail that they can be used in sessions as effectively as if they were living, breathing, human beings, as described below. For example, a child on the spectrum may know far more about Harry Potter, or about an actor in a specific movie, or about a character in a story, than she knows about Mom or Dad, or any living human being. It is very easy for individuals on the Spectrum to slip between reality and fantasy, and imagine that they are in the same world that the characters they imagine inhabit. Children generally have heroes, and spend years where they idolize characters from stories or favorite videos. However, as they grow up and realize that these people are not real, they come to a realization that Spiderman cannot truly climb buildings, Superman cannot really fly, and the Little Mermaid is just a character. Eventually, and with some coaxing at times, most children on the Autism Spectrum stop looking for these characters to be present in public.

However, some children do not make the distinction that their fantasy heroes are non-real. It is a short mental leap for them from time to time, from the real world to the dream world. Therefore, they may be terribly upset by their dreams. If someone whom they love and trust hurts or betrays them in a dream, people on the Autism Spectrum may project anger upon that person when awake. However, they may expect that the person "at fault" knows why they are angry, and that they are justified in their anger. They make no distinction between the two realms of dreaming and waking. No wonder the innocent person who is the target of such anger is dumbfounded.

Jessica originally had difficulty distinguishing fact from fiction, but the strategies I have described have eliminated even this issue. As mentioned repeatedly, perception is the key to everything. Jessica and I collected a wide variety of characters to talk about in our daily therapy sessions. Literary figures ranging from Hercules and Winnie the Pooh to some of the Teenage Mutant Ninja Turtles from the television series were added to real-life figures from the news and our own world. We talked about dozens of characters. Why did we like that person or character? What qualities did he possess that made us want to be like him, or what qualities made us not want to be like him? Now the biggie: Are they real people or fantasy creatures?

Jessica began writing stories around the age of 5, and her stories starred a superhero named Amy. Amy is short for Amelios, who is a boy. Jessica's Amy stories are nothing short of incredible, and the character of Amy possesses a lot of qualities that Jessica has been able to draw upon in her own life. Amy has amazing adventures, is brave, and saves the day with some regularity. Hence, the whole superhero status thing. Jessica and I have had several discussions about the dividing line between fantasy and reality and have used her stories as a guideline. The stories that she writes, and the characters within them, are fantasy. That entire world is of her making. All of that is fantasy. It has helped tremendously to have a starting point for her to be able to know what is real and what is not real.

One afternoon during the ninth grade, I was able to ask her:

Me: "Jessica, the conversation you had with the boy on the bus today, was that real or did you imagine it? I know you were upset because you thought he was mad at you."

Jessica: "Mom, I swear he looked mad, but he didn't say anything to me. He must have been mad about something else. "

Me: "Well, at first you said that he called you a name. Why did you say that?"

Jessica: "I thought he did. But I imagined it. It was kind of a daydream. I'm just having a bad day."

Me: "Are you doing okay? What's up with you?"

Jessica: "Mom, don't freak out. He calls people names all the time. I expected him to do the same to me, but he didn't. I was sort of afraid that he would. In my head, I heard all the bad stuff that he had said before he said anything, and then he didn't say anything at all. I got all weirded out. He didn't say anything to me at all. I don't even think he was mad at me at all now."

Me: "And so you're clear on what really happened on the bus? Do you have anything else you want to talk about? Any other things about the day you need to clear up?"

Jessica: "Nope, just homework and the usual crap."

Me: "Okay, but let me know if you need me to help you work out situations on the bus if they get ugly. Otherwise, I will let you handle it. Just keep being yourself. You've got it!"

When distinguishing between fantasy and reality, you can use whatever happens to surface in your conversation to build your child's self-esteem. Point out your child's strengths. Even if your child is nonverbal, remember that she is listening to you.

I did something similar with my stepson Averie in the fourth grade when talking with him about one of his heroes, a young man named Yugi who duels bad guys with trading cards. I mentioned that I would rather have Averie on my side because he was good at math, and that was something that was really useful. Averie hadn't given much thought to the fact that he might be better at something than his idol. "Besides that," I added, "you are a real live person and Yugi is a cartoon." Averie nodded in agreement, proud of his achievements in math.

With Jessica, she was able to accept who she was, and enjoy being the person that she is, by realizing that while she could not deflect bullets with magic bracelets like Wonder Woman, she had many talents that were special. Jessica and I examined what her talents were, and set about developing them. This viewpoint is crucial to all of us. A sense of self-worth is fundamental for everyone's happiness and well-being. For someone on the Autism Spectrum, the sense of "self" can be disconnected, or at the very least distorted. Learning one's place in the world is, therefore, extremely important.

In many ways, you cannot learn what your place is in the world until you have analyzed the world around you. We have seen the following storyline on television, and read about it in books, over and over and over: The country mouse and the city mouse don't do well in one another's environment. They simply don't know how to survive at first. What generally happens, and the lesson that these stories teach, is all about the adaptation of the species. If you cannot adapt, or if you refuse to adapt to changes in your environment or to changes in your life, you will inevitably have significant problems. Life is about change. Life is chaotic.

In many cases, children on the Autism Spectrum are left alone to their routines, and their caretakers are enslaved to the routines. This happens because they may be unwilling to take up the fight. In some cases, it may not seem worth the fight. It is never easy to fight. My argument is that a routine is fine if there is no other option. In Jessica's case, there was proof that she could learn to break the routine. She was capable of learning other patterns.

The following is a stellar example of Jessica's ability to break the routine. We went to Japan for a couple of years. After many years of going to school every day in a car, or on a bus the last year, she would now be walking to school. In Japan, this was the norm. Japanese children wear yellow hats and red backpacks, and walk, alone, to school, starting from age 5. We did not live far from the school compared to other children. Jessica did not have to take the train. But she had to cross the highway alone. She did not like this new independence, and I didn't either, frankly, but it was a case of "when in Rome ..."

Jessica adapted beautifully. She walked to and from school, in the rain, and in the snow, six days a week, in the year-round school schedule. She was very brave. When she arrived home, she let herself into our apartment, called me at work to let me know that she had arrived safely, told me about her day, and then cooked herself a hot snack. Often, I would ask her to do a few chores to help out, and I would tell her where to find the home schooling worksheets that I had prepared for her. She completed her fourth and fifth grades in Japan.

She was allowed to progress at her own pace, as long as she was progressing. Being able to progress at one's own pace is important. She is a kid first. She is a kid who never learned how to ride a two-wheeled bicycle. She learned how to ride a scooter, so she can balance on two wheels, and she had a scooter in Japan, but riding a bike wasn't important to her, and she was a bit afraid of it, so she was never pushed to learn to ride a bike. Frankly, we were always dealing with other issues, and before we left for Japan, I didn't feel comfortable turning her loose to ride alone anywhere. Instead, we went hiking, and we conquered an irrational fear of heights by climbing the walls at the local climbing gym. She went rappelling, and ended up climbing Mt. Fuji as well as several other mountains. She is very brave, and knows about getting outside her comfort zone.

If allowed to continue with her "comfortable" routine, she would still have few options available to her. We continue to work, and she progresses at her own pace. If a child who needed physical therapy protested against stretching her legs, you would continue the therapy if the end result would be that the child would be able to walk. You have to keep the goals in mind, and remember that you know your child better than anyone.

People will tell you many things about your children. Professionals have a lot of advice. Teachers may believe that they have your kids all figured out. Neighbors, friends, clergy, family members, folks on television, strangers at the grocery store, the list goes on and on when it comes to the multitudes of people who will tell you how to raise your children. Bur it all ends with the parent. You know your child. You must set some realistic goals. While you are doing that, set some pie-in-the-sky goals, too. Chances are, what actually happens will be in between the two.

Nearly every parent of a child with special needs has a story involving a family member or a close friend who took them aside in the days following the diagnosis and asked quite personal questions or gave allegedly well-meaning advice about how to address their child's challenges. My husband has a close relative who denied Averie's diagnosis. "There's nothing wrong with that boy that a butt-whipping wouldn't fix" was his comment on Averie's condition. Every time my husband tells that story in a room full of Spectrum Parents, he finds somebody with a similar tale to tell. Similarly, I have a close relative who took me to lunch, and lovingly but firmly detailed all the many reasons why I needed to put Jessica in an institution. This would not be the only time that I had to defend my position with her. I had to look into the eyes of these well-meaning family members and friends, and explain that we were working towards a goal: to give Jessica the best possible life – a life with purpose, one that she could be proud of!

I had Jessica's best interest in my heart at all times. I would never harm my child. I would never cause her pain. But I knew that she needed to be pushed. With a great deal of patience and an unending supply of love and attention, she and I worked nearly every moment we were together on some aspect of her therapy. From the very beginning, from the time of diagnosis age 4, every moment has been a teaching moment.

Helping her to understand the world around her has not been easy. So many individuals on the Autism Spectrum seem to be aloof. In Jessica's case it stems from a complete lack of attention to the world around her. After she had spent so much time in her own world, introducing her to the world around her was very much like bringing her to a foreign country. Part of our therapy involved using a book of Norman Rockwell pictures. I have always thought that Rockwell was a genius at capturing a moment. You can look at one of his pictures and immediately get the meaning, but you need a thousand words to tell the story behind it. As part of our therapy, I would sit with Jessica and look at a picture; I would say nothing while she looked at it. We began this during her second grade year when she was 7 years old. Usually she would laugh at the pictures and then study them. After a couple of minutes I would ask her to tell about what was happening in the picture.

Two pictures stick out in my mind as good examples. One is a picture of teenagers at a dance. In the foreground, it is obvious that a boy and girl have been dancing together, and he has stepped on her foot. She is holding her foot and frowning. He is embarrassed and wears an apologetic expression. His friends are in the background laughing and pointing at him.

Jessica looked at this picture and said that the boys were laughing because somebody told a joke. The girl was holding her foot because her shoes were too small and they hurt her feet. She was mad at the boy because he was making fun of her shoes. Clearly, she needed to be taught to see the situation again, and see the most probable scenario. At the same time, it is important to give credibility to her version. "That's a possibility. You were smart to see those clues," I would say. "But there's another answer that might be more likely. Let's look at it again."

The other example is a picture of boys running away from a sign that says "No Swimming." They are carrying their clothing, with water drops flying off their bodies. Your thought processes just went from A to E. We "know" that these boys got caught swimming and are running away, maybe from somebody carrying a broom and yelling at them to get out of his cistern!

Jessica looked at the picture and said that the boys were going swimming; that they were on their way to the pool. I pointed out the wet hair and the flying drops of water. She explained it was sweat. It was a hot day. I pointed out that the expressions on the boys' faces suggested fear. They didn't look happy to be going swimming. They look scared. She frowned. I waited. She still didn't get it. Then I pointed to the sign. After much fidgeting, she finally understood that they got caught and were fleeing the scene of the crime.

Deductive reasoning skills are important, but they are hard to learn for most of us. For the Autistic mind, they are extremely elusive. Being able to analyze the environment gives individuals with Autism the power to identify the things within the environment that need to be controlled. They may be better able to judge what clothing is appropriate to wear for the season. They may remember to take an umbrella when it is raining. They are more able to judge when something is wrong and determine whether or not they can fix it.

Being able to judge and put into context what's going on is essential for safety and everyday living. If you were to walk into a room where a person is obviously distressed and crying, and the source of that distress was a criminal who was making an escape after having pulled a weapon on that person, most of us would naturally seek a safe place for ourselves, and for the distressed person if we could do so without causing further danger. A person with Autism might walk past someone who had just been shot, unaware that she was in danger. She may misunderstand what is happening, decide it is a game, and chase the fleeing criminal. She may ignore what is happening, and go about her own routine. She may see what has happened, process it as being wrong but be unable to act accordingly. She may talk to the person who is distressed, and expect that he will be calm. Higher-functioning individuals on the Autism Spectrum may be able to dial 9-1-1 and get help, but be so distraught that they are unable to speak clearly to the operator. It would be a safe bet that if shrieking is part of their typical behavioral repertoire, they will shriek a bit if agitated. This might alert the criminal and put the person with Autism directly in harm's way.

The list of potential problems is clear. Other problems include what to do when in a fire or other kind of accident. In number of cases a person with Autism was killed as a result of his or her inability to know how to react in an emergency situation. Many children with Autism have "hideouts" where they feel safe. Often, they retreat to these places when alone or scared. For example, when children awake with nightmares during the night, they often find such places in the early hours of the morning, when their parents are asleep. Similarly, in an emergency situation, they become afraid and may retreat to their safety hideouts, and then the emergency staff, police, firefighters and medics have trouble locating them. Calling to them will do no good. Many Spectrum individuals are nonverbal, or have limited verbal clarity when afraid. Others shut down, and simply shriek or rock in place. Still others do not respond at all to a stranger, whether or not that stranger is attempting to be of help.

Therefore, many children and adults on the Autism Spectrum have been injured or killed because emergency personnel were unable to reach them in time. Emergency personnel are faced with many challenges when they arrive on the scene, and many tragedies may be avoided if parents and caretakers of individuals on the Autism Spectrum help emergency personnel in the community identify these individuals and how they might best be rescued or comforted in emergency situations. With the number of Autism cases on the rise, it is a emergency response issue that must be addressed.

As she progressed as a result of our therapy, Jessica quickly became a child who knew no strangers. This was good in that she learned which people she should talk to, as in authority figures she could trust, like the police or the school nurse. However, it took a little TOO well in one respect. I had to be careful that she was aware of her surroundings, and I could not take any lesson for granted. Every new situation was a new lesson to be learned. If she brought forth knowledge that was learned from a previous lesson, to be used in association with whatever we were discussing, I praised her profusely. But I didn't take any prior knowledge for granted. Every learning situation started from scratch. Soon, she learned how to talk to everyone easily. By being able to adapt more easily to her environment, and being more flexible with regard to her surroundings, she is much more likely to be successful in our world. And that's what it's been about from the very beginning – preparing my child to be successful in the world.

CHAPTER ELEVEN

Going to School

"To Mainstream or Not to Mainstream ... That Is the Question."

Inclusion has been the topic of some discussion at every Autism-related conference I have ever attended. Indeed, the federal government and the educational community do not always agree, as reflected in changing policies. The community is full of questions.

How much time should Jessica spend in a general education classroom? How much exposure to typical children should she have? At the beginning, these questions were much more difficult to answer. Today, we live a "typical" life, whatever that means. Life is what it is. I happen to believe that life is what you make it. We are proof of that.

When Jessica and I first began visiting doctors, trying to determine why she was losing her vocabulary, years before she was diagnosed with Autism, I suspected that it was a hearing problem. I wanted to get the malfunction under control, in plenty of time for her to adjust so that she could start school on time with her peers.

That was the goal: "to start school on time with her peers." It was important to me. Parents don't always think about it actively, but it's important. Downplay it if you want, but think about it. When you were growing up, you were excited about turning another year older. It made you another year cooler. You were another year wiser. Admit it – you were another year better than the kids in the grade below you. Getting another year bigger was a huge deal, and we all got really excited about it.

Think about what it is like in elementary school for a minute. When you move to the next grade, it is a huge milestone. Each year you are in school, you get to go to birthday parties for your friends. All the rest of the kids at school know how old everybody is becoming on their birthdays. You know which kids are turning older first. You know, especially in smaller communities, which kids in your class are the "older kids," and which are the "younger kids." One year in the maturity level of a child can make a tremendous difference in his life, which is why people debate so much about allowing children to skip grades. There are instances where it can be done successfully, and there are students who can do so gracefully. Others shouldn't attempt skipping a grade at all.

On the other hand, there are kids on the Autism Spectrum who are not ready to move on to the next grade. I have worked with a number of students and their parents in such situations. "Watering down" curriculum, or modifying the educational standards may not be the best way to handle the situation. A meeting of the parents, teachers, and therapists is essential, in order to determine what assignments the student should be expected to complete. If the parents and the school faculty are working together as a team, things go much smoother for any child, whether on the Autism Spectrum or not. Every year, I was forced to think about retention in the event that Jessica hit some plateau and was unable to progress. I talked about it with several teachers, and in an attempt to preserve her dignity, we agreed that it is often easier to retain a child when the rest of the peer group is going to another school, for example, at the end of the fifth grade when the class will be going on to the sixth grade in another school across town.

I can hear the elementary school teachers grumble. Bear with me for a moment: If a child is struggling in the fourth grade and must repeat a grade in elementary school, it may be better if he repeats the fifth grade than the fourth. Repeating the fourth grade will invite a social stigma from the peer group that may inhibit learning. Repeating the fifth grade, on the other hand, is an easier transition in many ways.

The point is that when we were in elementary school, we all knew which kids in our grade weren't "ready" to start school on time. They were "slow." Maybe they were just a little delayed in their progress, but it was a very significant social stigma for those kids. These were not special education students. These were kids like everyone else in the class, only they were a year older than everyone else.

Kids can be cruel to each other. There is no other way to say it. I wanted Jessica to start school on time, or to start early, if possible. I wanted to give her every possible chance to excel. I didn't want to give any of the other kids any ammunition against her, like her being a year older because she "wasn't ready to start on time with her peers."

I hear parents talking about what kind of "learning disorder" their children have, as if their kids have some malady that prevents them from learning. This malady is often used as an excuse for why the child cannot perform at school, and to justify why the child should be excused from normal activities, such as physical education or extracurricular activities, band, volunteerism, or being a contributing member of society like everyone else. Many of these people do absolutely nothing to help their children learn to live their own lives with purpose. They leave it up to the special education teachers, and take no responsibility upon themselves.

I understand that there are "true" learning disabilities. Autism is one of them. I hear the cries of parents everywhere, and I sympathize. ADD, ADHD, dyslexia … the list goes on … makes it difficult to learn in the "traditional" manner. Teachers in today's classroom have to modify the learning environment to reach the students. Students have to work twice as hard to learn half as much, it would seem. Parents must realize that to be abreast of what their children are learning, or not learning, in school, has much to do with whether or not they are aware of what is being taught in the classroom. All parents are busy; but we must talk to our children. We must be aware of what's going on at school. It is our duty as parents. I recognize Autism is a type of learning disability. However, if your child has a learning disability, and you tell her that she has a learning disability, she will always see herself in that way. There will be a barrier in every classroom between the child and the teacher, before every lesson begins.

As Jessica began to progress, and it became evident that there was nothing wrong with her mental capability, that, in fact, she was advanced in the way that she processed many things, I changed my perception permanently, including changing my language about "learning disorder" when it came to Jessica and her Autism.

Teachers would call me before the start of a new school year to inquire about Jessica's "condition." Many were apprehensive about Autism. Some years, she was shuffled from classroom to classroom. I was told by a principal one year that a certain teacher had "a lot of experience with mental retardation and other conditions, so Jessica should have a good time in her class. You will like her," he concluded. Hanging up the phone that afternoon, my heart was heavy. It was clear that few had a clear understanding of the Autism Spectrum. People were still afraid. To such people, I quickly point out that my child does not have a learning disorder, but "disordered learning." She can and will learn, but in a way that is different from others. She will be struggling, most likely, but just wait. Soon, she will get her bearings and then she'll take off.

Mainstreaming is important for a number of reasons. The need for socialization is the primary reason. Jessica would not learn to become comfortable in a typical learning environment if she was forever stuck in a resource classroom or the self-contained classroom where she started preschool. That much is easy to understand. Somehow I had to get her into general education classes.

To do so meant convincing the school district and administration that she would not be a distraction to the regular schedule of the teacher, or a danger to the other students. I wish I could tell you that this was an easy thing to do. It was not. However, because I have done it, and because I have made mistakes doing it, I can advise others on what not to do, and can give tips on how to do it the right way.

I mentioned early on that I enrolled Jessica in a regular kindergarten, without an IEP so that she would not have to wear a helmet. I was working hard to eliminate the other distractive behaviors. I knew that if I could eliminate these behaviors, and find the right teachers for our team, we'd have it made. I started teacher shopping.

We had to change kindergartens in the middle of the school year because of behavior difficulties. It was heartbreaking, because I loved that little school, but better leave than risk worse difficulties later. I took Jessica to a church school not far from Methodist College, where I worked. She finished kindergarten there, and by that time I had found the program I wanted for her for first-grade year.

Cumberland County Schools was going to attempt an Autism class at Alma Easom Elementary School in downtown Fayetteville, North Carolina. I met with the teacher for the class. She and I talked about Jessica's proposed IEP, and some goals for mainstreaming into regular classroom settings. We were on the same team. With that in mind, I began looking for a house in the neighborhood. We made a cross-town move to enable Jessica to attend this school.

That first-grade year was great for Jessica. The teacher in her class and the full-time aide were both very good with her, and they worked with my regimen well, sending home notes daily at my request. I was able to keep my records and continue our daily therapy. Jessica was enrolled in speech therapy and occupational therapy as well. She continued to make progress at an astounding rate. The mainstreaming into a general education class from the self-contained Autism classroom happened quickly as a result of my working together with the teacher. Jessica and I worked on the behavioral aspects of her Autism, and this allowed her to attend regular classes with her peers without causing distractions. She loved school and adored her teachers. She was a good student, and had the reputation of wanting to please. She responded well to being praised for her efforts. She was mainstreamed into a math class, where she did very well. The math teacher's recommendation got her into the science class. Those teachers helped move her into social studies. It wasn't long before she was only "checking in" at the Autism classroom as her home base, to let the teacher help her with organizational tasks. She did so well that it was clear that she would be able to manage on her own for the next year, if we adults on her team could manage to convince the administration to allow it.

I fought the school district every year. Most of my battles had to do with professionals who recognized the label of Autism, instead of recognizing my child as a student. There was a constant fight to keep Jessica out of the self-contained class. There were frequent complaints of having to spend time redirecting Jessica's attention. Teachers would notice that Jessica was distracted, and have to say "Jessica, pay attention." Perhaps they would have to say this once or twice during the course of the class. They would get tired of saying this. I get tired of it myself. I understand. It wouldn't take long each year before somebody in the school would suggest that Jessica might be more comfortable in a resource classroom. They would remind me that she was Autistic.

They would tell me about the challenges of teaching children with special needs. At each meeting, I would sit patiently and let them enlighten me. Then I would tell them what I wanted them to do for my child. If they were not prepared to do the right thing, I was prepared to move her to another school where the team would be more receptive.

On the few occasions when teachers complained about my child, I was ready to defend her with any ammunition I could think of. I appealed to their sense of devotion as teachers. How could they not want to make a difference for her? How could they not want to do the right thing? I killed them with kindness. I'll admit to bringing cookies to some and showering them with attention. Only once did a faculty member cause me to remind her that Jessica has a right to the same education as every other child, and that to remove her from the class would take legal action. I said so with a lawyer at my side and a smile on my face.

Mainstreaming is crucial, not only to the Autistic student, but also to the non-Autistic children in the classroom. The Autistic child needs to be conditioned to act in an appropriate manner, certainly. The others need to be tolerant. Mainstreaming is the only way to go, for the benefit of all concerned.

The children in Jessica's classrooms were lucky to have her in there with them. She was a daily lesson in tolerance. She was also the most attentive child to the likes and dislikes of her classmates. She remembered everyone's birthday, and all their favorite colors and snacks. Besides, she worked very, very hard at her schoolwork.

For any child, it takes more than what's being taught at school to make a well-rounded education. This is especially important for kids on the Autism Spectrum who have difficulty processing what is given to them in the traditional classroom. They may need to take what is offered and then see it applied in the world around them. I supplemented what was happening at school with computer programs at home and lots of extra reading. We took field trips to places to talk about things. We spent time at the library. We went to the art museum. I took her to concerts at the college because they were free to me as an employee. We went to see a lot of plays. We talked constantly. Everything was constantly being analyzed.

A good example of our processing things all the time would be when we took a trip to the art museum and were looking at Impressionists. Jessica was studying art in her fourth-grade class, and she had learned about Monet, but hadn't seen any of the art except in the textbook.

I deliberately walk with her very close to the wall, and stand with her, very close to the painting. As we look at the painting, I ask:

"Jessica, what do you see?"

"Dots. Just dots. Dots of color. Blobs."

"Yep. Does it look like anything?"

"It looks like blobs," she repeats.

"Okay," I say. "We are going to turn around and walk five steps away, and then look at it again. I think you will get a surprise. Don't turn around until I do. Ready? Go."

We count five steps, and turn around together, and when she looks, she gasps and says: "WOW! Flowers! A girl! A girl is there! How did you do that? Do it again!"

We do this to two more paintings. The third time, I tell her that I have a secret. The secret is that you have to look at most things twice, or even three times, to see what is really there. Sometimes you have to look at them a different way, or from farther away, to figure them out. It's not just about art. It's about people, about problems, about literature, about the things we read about in the newspaper, about relationships, and about most things in life. If something just looks like blobs, and doesn't make much sense, try looking at it in a different way. I also tell her that I love the way that she looks at the world. She takes my hand. It's a great day at the museum.

I realize that this is a fourth-grade example, and that's a little ahead of where I am in the story. Back during the first-grade days, she was still very echolalic and she was struggling in everything that she did. However, she had a brilliant way of looking at things, and it was different from the way that most other people looked at the world. She was always very interested in art, and in creating her own artwork. One of the first indications to me that she had a talent for seeing things in creative ways happened the summer before her first-grade year. She was coloring a picture for me in my office at Methodist College. I made many copies on white paper of one picture that Jessica liked, which was a drawing of a car with people inside it. I kept these pictures with a box of crayons in my office, and Jessica was able to get them and create artwork whenever she liked. One afternoon, she was hard at work for almost an hour, and then brought me a creation that I thought was interesting. She handed it to me, and I glanced at it, ready with my usual comment of "Oh Jessica, how pretty!" But the paper that she handed me of a car and the people had no color at all. I must have looked confused.

"Jessica, what's this?" I asked.

Jessica turns the paper over to show me that the other side of the paper had been colored in many shades of blue and green, with lots of scribbling. It looked like what she used to create in preschool. I was confused, but I gave her a good one:

"How pretty!"

"No." She said and took the paper from me. Then she walked over to the window in my office and held it up so that the picture of the car and the people could be seen. The light shone through the window, and through the colors that she had drawn on the back of the paper, and shaded in the car and the people on the front side of the paper. She had colored the picture from the "other" side.

"WHOA! That's incredible, Jessica! You are amazing! That is beautiful!"

Jessica nodded her head. "I know." She said. "It's for you."

I kept that "blank" picture on my bulletin board in my office for many years. Every time someone would ask about it, I would have the opportunity to show them how Jessica saw the world.

I insisted that she be given the chance to fully mainstream for the second grade, and the first-grade teacher backed my request. I admit that there were many among the family, the therapists, and teachers who were holding their breath and hoping for the best. My words were "The worst that can happen is that we have to go back to a home base in resource. Big deal. The best that can happen is that she's in second grade on time."

The best happened. Jessica attended second grade at Long Hill Elementary with a good teacher. It was a combined class of second and third graders. Some days, Jessica was able to do third-grade work. The older kids were so good to her. The influence of their behavior, and the level of tolerance that they showed to her was incredible. It was a fabulous year for her.

Third grade was College Lakes Elementary. Jessica stayed in a mainstream environment. She learned how to function there. By this time, she was well established in our therapy regimen at home, and her teacher did her best to help keep up with our records. Jessica did well in her class.

Shortly thereafter, I was hired by the Consulate General of Japan to teach English. So we went to Japan for two years. Jessica spent two years being home schooled in Japan, but attended the local Japanese elementary school for non-language-intensive courses such as art, music, home economics, mathematics, physical science, drama and physical education. She became fully functional in the Japanese language and in Japanese culture. I supplemented these subjects at home, and also taught her English, literature, poetry, American and world history, geography, earth science, biology, music history, art history and life skills.

In other words, Jessica went to Japanese elementary school with her Japanese friends Monday through Saturday. When she came home in the afternoon, she would go to school at night with me, and on the weekends too. When she and I returned to the States two years later, after she had completed the fourth and fifth grades in Japan, and the fourth and fifth grades in home schooling from me, we had her tested for the public schools. She tested at the tenth-grade level.

First, because of Jessica's maturity, her level of experience in the world and her life knowledge, I made the decision that skipping the sixth grade would benefit her. First of all, it would save her a year of social torment at the mercy of junior high school girls. Second, she did not have a peer group that knew her prior to her departure, so there would be only "new friends" to make in her new grade. Had there been a grade full of peers to be left behind, to watch her move ahead and look on with resentment as the years progressed, it might have been a factor. Finally, she was physically the same size as those girls, and was reaching puberty. It was time.

As before, I went to a small setting to initiate her re-entry to mainstreaming. I found a small private Catholic school with very high standards, and enrolled her in the seventh grade. She made friends quickly with the girls on the basketball team, and played ball that year. She had never played basketball before, and the Blue Angels were patient with her as she learned. They were a very good team, coming in second in the league championship that year. I sat on the sidelines at every game, screaming my head off and waving blue and white pompoms. I was struck from time to time by how odd it was that Jessica was out there on that court, playing a game that was so spontaneous and fast. It would be an overload for so many kids with Autism. And yet – there she was! I was there at every game, to scream at the top of my lungs and wave my cheesy pompoms. "Number 24, that's my daughter – look at her – there she is! Go Jazz! Go baby- YEAH!!!"

I get emotional when I remember times like that. I can't help it. She didn't make a shot all year. But that didn't matter. What did matter was that she took some shots. She attempted to make some. She was out there. She ran, and blocked and assisted. She was an essential member of the team. They liked her and they needed her. She didn't warm the bench. She wore a uniform, and she played.

Towards the end of the season, the coach's wife and I were sitting next to one another at a game, discussing Jessica. I mentioned how great the coach was with all the girls. I said Jessica really liked him, and that I felt this was important because so many kids with Autism have trust issues.

"What are you talking about?" She asked me.

"Jessica is Autistic," I said.

"No, she is not," she said with obvious disbelief and shock on her face.

"Yes, she is," I countered proudly.

"I never would have known it," she finally acknowledged.

"That's the way we like it. We don't mind that people know it. We would just rather tell you about it than you be able to see it," I concluded with a smile.

I have a lot of similar conversations with people who have known Jessica for a long time. Some admit that they picked up on something that seemed "a little odd." Okay. We're all a little odd in some ways. Besides, Jessica is 15 – some of that oddness will fade as she matures. I know that I was completely wacky at 15. I rather like her oddness. If she remains as "odd" as she is today, she is no more odd than anyone else.

Her friends from high school are neurotypical, non-Autistic friends. She is back in the public school setting. She left Catholic school after seventh grade, and spent eighth grade at Northwood Middle School. Ninth grade is high school. It was difficult to watch her get on the bus for high school, but we did all the right shopping for high schools.

Mills University Studies High School is ranked #20 in the nation by *Newsweek*. Jessica is part of the broadcasting program, and is doing well in her academic courses. The students and teachers tend to be serious and committed. Mills also has a very good advanced placement program. She rides a bus more than an hour to get there every morning and an hour to get home in the afternoon. But it isn't a waste of time. It gives her time to study. She's an honor student, and was recently inducted into the National Honor Society. She is a junior this year.

Mainstreaming was tough. I knew that getting Jessica's behavior in check to eliminate the behaviors that were typically Autistic, and ultimately distracting to the teaching environment, would be a challenge, but it was a fight I was willing to take up. As with every other aspect of the regimen presented here, you decide how far you are willing to go. You can camp at the base of the mountain, or you climb to the summit. Take it from me and Jessica: It's a little tough at times, and the switchbacks can be a tricky, but the view is a lot better from the top.

CHAPTER TWELVE

Learning Strategies

"We Run Before We Walk Sometimes"

To say that the Autistic mind works a little differently might be an understatement. I have said to my daughter over and over that there is nothing wrong with the way that her mind processes information. It's simply a little different from the way most other people process the same information.

When she was being tested for Autism, she was given a series of diagnostics, all aimed at measuring the many ways she handles input. It is easy to illustrate this type of test. Imagine three different-colored bowls. You have a red bowl, a yellow bowl, and a blue bowl. They are all empty. In front of these bowls is a pile of poker chips in the same three colors, all mixed together. Your task is to get all the red chips into the red bowl, all the yellow chips into the yellow bowl, and all the blue chips into the blue bowl. How would you do it?

Take a moment to think about how you would complete that task. The truly efficient people and the organizers among you will stack up the colors in order and throw them into their respective bowls. The creative people among you will imagine picking up a handful of the chips and dropping a red here and a yellow there. Now drop two blues, and another red. You are losing patience. Pick up three or four reds and drop those in the red bowl all at once. Now get a few yellows and put those in the yellow bowl. Now you decide to get all the blues. Then you get a few reds in one hand and a few yellows in the other. If any of the above descriptions comes close to how you might complete the task, your choice falls among the most popular.

The Autistic mind works a little differently. Jessica will pick up one red at a time – Red. Red. Red. Red. Red – until they are completed. Then she will move on to the yellow – Yellow. Yellow. Yellow – and so on, until the task is done. There is a specific sequence. In Jessica's way of thinking, that's the only way the task can be done.

In some ways Jessica's method is very thorough. I make certain that I tell her this each time it comes to my attention. It is important when administering therapy of the kind discussed here that you give credit to the child's way of thinking, and then provide an alternative way. If there is a "work smarter, not harder" way of doing it, that's fantastic. I am careful to try to preserve Jessica's feelings about her thinking process-es. I frequently try to get her to "think outside the box," to skip steps in that sequential thinking pattern, in order to prevent a "loop" that ulti-mately could result in an emotional storm.

I began this chapter with the premise of running before we walk. It seems ridiculous to even surmise that this could be possible. However, when Jessica found her words, I soon discovered that she could read. Labeling everything in our house had made an impression. When English was what was required of her, her vocabulary began to show in full force.

Learning things in reverse order became more the norm for us than the exception. Let's go back to the night I tossed eggs on my kitchen floor. Jessica didn't know that an egg would break because she had never seen an egg break before. She didn't have that experience in her knowl-edge base. She saw the broken egg, and could go "backward" a few seconds and see the egg in my hand. (We talked about this experience, and I used variations of this exercise quite a bit.)

"Look at what you have. You have a broken egg. Why do you have a broken egg? You have a broken egg because you dropped it."

Now you are not dealing with an "if-then" statement. You are dealing with "why" and "because," cause and effect. It is a completely different situation. It is another essential level of understanding necessary to succeed in the world around us.

Many Autistic minds have trouble learning because they are frustrated with the order in which they are required to learn. Jessica had tremendous trouble learning how to add, for example. She could not do it. The addition symbol (+) looked like a lower-case "t" to her. She read it as a "t," and, therefore, saw no mathematical relevance. She was lost. Word problems were no different. The entire concept was lost and she was frustrated. I was frustrated, too.

I was administering Jessica's therapy one afternoon. As often before, our Barbies were talking to one another. One Barbie had asked another Barbie a question. The second Barbie did not know the answer, and said "Hmmmmm." While we waited for Barbie to think of an answer, I sang the theme from *Jeopardy*, because Jessica loves music, and the musical breaks helped to keep her attention. I love *Jeopardy*. The answers are the questions. You think in reverse order.

Suddenly it hit me – reverse the order! I tried a couple of the word problems out, using apples or candy. Sure enough, using subtraction, I was able to teach Jessica all about how to manipulate numerals. Subtraction was easy for her. She understood it very well. She was able to look at what you have, then take something away, and see what was left. That made sense to her.

Once subtraction was done, flipping the sign around and teaching addition was a snap. Suddenly Jessica was empowered. She felt like she owned the math world after that. It was, and still is, difficult, when she has to learn new concepts. The traditional teaching strategies don't always make sense to her.

It was much the same when she had to learn multiplication and division. She learned division first. After division was mastered, multiplication was simple. The subject of multiplication brings to mind another strategy I employed with Jessica. As mentioned, I used music in her therapy at every possible opportunity. When learning multiplication, like many kids, Jessica would have to take weekly tests, called time trials. These would consist of one hundred simple multiplication problems to be completed in five minutes.

Even though Jessica knew the answers to every question, she would bring home grades ranging between 30% and 40% on the time trials. When looking at her tests, it was clear that all the problems were correct. She was obviously becoming distracted and not completing the test in the allotted time. I asked her teacher for a sample of the trials so I could observe her testing style at home. Then, I looked for a piece of music that was less than five minutes long. I found a Mozart minuet that I thought she would like. I played it for her over and over; and we also sang the tune together.

Then I played it for Jessica while making her take a practice test. The rule was that she had to only look at her paper and concentrate on the music and the math. Nothing else could be in her mind. At the end of the music, I took up her paper. She had completed more than 80 problems correctly. We celebrated. Then we tried again. It took several attempts for Jessica to master concentrating on the music and the math problems only. We called this minuet her "magic math music."

My instruction to Jessica was that she was to start the music in her head when it was time to begin a test like this. Two weeks later, she brought home a multiplication time trial with 100%, GREAT JOB and a huge smiley face scrawled in red pen across the top. Here was the proof that she could learn. She simply learned in a different order than those around her. Different isn't bad; it's just different. Different takes patience, that's all.

When Jessica and I lived in Japan I supplemented the learning she received at the local elementary school with English language courses at home. I documented all that we did in Japan in my letters home. In a letter to my mother, I wrote of teaching Jessica some basic algebra techniques. This is a good example of how her mind "hangs" on minor details instead of moving on to the important information that she needs to process. Jessica was 10 years old at the time I wrote the following letter.

Yesterday we were tackling word problems in math. It's still easy stuff, but I am training her to do it in her head. It went a little something like this …

"Jessica," I began, *"you are going to the store with three of your closest friends. You and Friend #2 have the same amount of money. Friend #3 has twice the amount of money you do. Friend #4 has one dollar less than Friend #3. Altogether you have a total of $14.00. How much money do YOU have?"*

Jessica: "What store?"

Me: "It doesn't matter. Any store ... like the Hyaku-en Plaza." (The Japanese equivalent of our dollar stores.)

Jessica: "They don't take dollars there."

Me: "It doesn't matter. The Dollar Store. There. The Dollar Store."

Jessica: "Mmmmmmm (thinking very hard)... So who is Friend #1?"

Me: "You are. You are Friend #1."

Jessica: "Why don't the others have names?"

Me: "They don't need names because it's a math problem."

Jessica: "But you said they are my closest friends. I should know their names."

Me: "Jessica. Stay with me. Math, honey. Math. We are doing a math problem. Okay. Give them some names if it will make it easier." (My fingers find the ridges in my brow line and rub them furiously.)

Jessica: "Okay. Tomoko-chan is Friend #2, Kaori is Friend #3. Ayaka can be Friend #4 even if she is kinda bossy."

Me: "Very good. Now. How much money do you have?"

Jessica: "But Mom, Tomo, Kaori and Ayaka probably don't have any dollars."

Me: "Math problem ... we are doing math ..."(eyes clamped shut)

Jessica: "Okay, sorry, now what was the problem again?"

Me: "I forget."

Well, I did resurrect the fried remains of the problem from the recesses of my poor brain and managed to write them down. When Jessica didn't get it on the second try, I suggested that I introduce her to a new concept called EKS (x).

Me: "You have EKS amount of dollars. Write that down."

Jessica: "I have x dollars."

Me: "Good. Now, how about Tomo-chan?"

Jessica: "Tomo-chan has x dollars."

Me: "Right. Now, Kaori?"

Jessica: "Kaori has x+x dollars."

Me: "Yes, you can also say 2 times x, and write it 2x."

Jessica: "Okay. How about Ayaka?"

Me: "You tell me."

Jessica: (lots of figuring, whispering, counting on fingers commences ... then the wiggling begins. I am losing her. MAYDAY!!! MAYDAY!!!)

Me: "How much does the problem say?"

Jessica: "... one dollar less than Kaori."

Me: "... and Kaori has ..."

Jessica: "2x dollars."

Me: "Right-o! So you can write that like 2x-1."

Jessica: "Oh! I see now. I have $2.50."

Me: "WHAT??????!!!!! When did you figure it all out?"

Jessica: "About that time I remembered that Kaori had 1 dollar more than Ayaka and twice as much as me and Tomo together, and 14 dollars is the perfect amount. That was an easy one. Give me another."

Me: "Hang on. I need a drink of water."

Jessica: (with a big smile) "Can I still be Friend #1?"

This is a good illustration of how Jessica's mind works. She is easily distracted by things that do not have any bearing on the final outcome. By the end of the exercise, I was able to help her do these types of problems and look only at the factors that she needed to consider, without giving names to extraneous friends and converting dollars to yen. Once those things are out of the way, it is easy for her brilliant mind to work its magic. As with most other struggles, it came down to simply being able to organize.

It was a struggle to get her organized. Organizational skills are hard for Auties. It was important that I stay out of Jessica's way at school as much as possible. When she entered eighth grade, I touched base with her teachers, and left them with my phone numbers, but then told them I would be out of the way as much as possible. I wanted to see how functional Jessica would be on her own as we prepared to send her into a high school environment, where I would have to be out of sight for social reasons.

Jessica usually worked hard on her homework but failed to turn her work in. Then, we would get near the end of the grading period and she would receive a terrible grade. I would be confused, because she would have been doing well in her work. A simple call to the teacher, asking him to check Jessica's notebook would rectify the situation. But Jessica wasn't the only child in that position. There were others, who were neurotypical, or non-Autistic, who had failed to turn in work. She got through the eighth grade, and her standardized testing had placed her well above average.

Jessica is fairly typical when it comes to organizational skills and study skills. She's flying on her own in high school. She's doing okay. I am proud of her efforts. She and I continue to work together, and she continues to improve. She knows that there is still much to be done, that she is still in a race, and she is still willing to take up that baton and run. We use that analogy often to motivate ourselves and to motivate Jessica. But she never is made to feel as if she is in a race against others, including her peers in her grade, although she is often near the top of her class. She is only racing herself. She is out there every day to do the very best that she can do. If she is doing her best, and giving her best effort, she should be satisfied, and we are satisfied. If that earns her an A, or a C or a D, it does not matter. If it is her best effort, we are proud of her and for her. Taking up the baton in the race against oneself takes guts, no matter what the race is.

Don't worry too much about what the teachers at your child's school tell you about his or her ability to keep up with the other students. I have been told that my daughter was mentally retarded. I have been told that she would be too much of a distraction to remain with regular children. I have been told that she would never keep up with her peers on her reading level.

When Jessica was 8, she explained to one of her teachers how Robert E. Lee made crucial mistakes at Gettysburg. When she was 9, she performed the balcony scene from *Romeo and Juliet* on a mission trip in Kentucky for talent night and received a standing ovation; she has a deep love for Shakespeare and an appreciation of his works. At 10, she could tell you why Monet's art was so important to the Impressionist movement. At 11, she was composing her own piano music. At 12, she directed a team of artists to put her work on buildings in town for the holidays.

At 13, the child they told me would never keep up with reading comprehension on her level read *Animal Farm* by George Orwell. She understood that it wasn't about animals. We had a wonderful discussion about it, and she'll even sum it up for you: "Power corrupts, but absolute power corrupts absolutely." Those of us who had to read it all had to learn it like this. She actually gets it. She was able to apply it to what's going on in the world, to the regime in Iraq, and was able to feel blessed by her American birthright.

At 14, she was writing her own stories, and was selected to be a member of Bobbi McKenna's Book Club for Authors, which is intended for adults.

At 15, she is a published author of an E-book submission on the Autism Today website, has been a keynote speaker for Arkansas Disability Awareness Day, Arkansas People First, Arkansas Disability Coalition, Beyond the Borders, Easter Seals Arkansas, and has spoken at the Autism Society of America's preconference. She will be releasing her own book within the next year. She is a remarkable child in every sense of the word.

Jessica was able to learn new strategies to process the information given to her. Sometimes it had to be given to her in reverse order. At other times it meant simply redirecting the attention away from what could have been an uncomfortable situation. At all times, it took a commitment to the goal, and a lot of patience. An interest in space travel, world folklore, molecular biology and elephants helps, too.

Remarkable Spectrum kids still display uneven skills, however. My remarkable Spectrum kid was no different. At every stage of the game, she has needed to ask the same question, over and over: "What are we doing now?" As she has matured, this question has evolved into "What are the plans for the day?" But it's the same thing. She has needed to know what's going on. Averie is the same way. Actually, Steve and I call Averie "20-Questions Man" for this very reason.

While having a handle on what is happening from one minute to the next can help individuals on the Spectrum feel in control, it can also be a miniature routine of sorts. If you decide to deviate from what you have told them, they may or may not be able to carry on with you.

Well, my kids can, but it's because they don't know what's coming next.

I answer the "What are we doing now" questions with a myriad responses that often have nothing to do with a shopping list or visiting Aunt Mary. Possible answers to the question "What are we doing now?" include:

"We are breathing. Isn't that great, Jessica? Breathing is a great thing. We breathe with our lungs. The air goes in and it gives oxygen to our blood. I like breathing. I do it all day long, and I don't even think about it. That's what we are doing right now. We are breathing."

OR

"We are walking. Later we will be doing something else; I am not sure what. Right now, we are walking. Let's do that for right now. We walk with our legs and feet, and we are the only mammals that walk upright all the time on two legs. Can you think of any other mammals that use two legs sometimes?"

OR

"We are planning space travel. I think it would be great to live on Mars. We went to the moon back in 1969, but it was only for a visit. The astronauts left a flag up there. Sometimes people say that they can see a man in the moon. The Japanese say that there is a rabbit in the moon. What do you think about that?"

OR

"We are thinking about elephants. They look very thoughtful. I always like watching elephants perform in the circus, but I don't like thinking about them all locked up in those cages. I like to think about them wild in Africa. Elephants have very big legs and very big ears. I wonder if they can hear far-away sounds with those big ears. What other animals do you like to think about?"

Jessica was always totally surprised at what would come out of my mouth when she asked what we were doing. She would, of course, be asking about the schedule, and I would be redirecting her attention to something much more random. It was a way of helping her loosen up. At first, she would fidget, until she understood whether I was teasing or was serious about the topic. She would laugh if the topic was something funny, and then join in the conversation.

This sounds very silly, I know. You have to get creative. Pick a letter of the alphabet and make the topic of your answer begin with that letter. Have an answer ready, because the question is coming. Be ready. If you are ready, you never know what good may come of it. It's all therapy.

In my general experience, people take themselves much too seriously, leading lives with too little humor. We have to learn to laugh at our situations, and at ourselves, if we are going to learn to cope with what life is dealing out. I was concerned that Jessica would become too stiff, and that humor would continue to be too elusive for her. So we laughed about everything. I purposely laughed at myself, and taught her how to laugh at me, too.

Lots of things that happen in life are funny. Our life, for the most part, has not been funny. At least, not "ha-ha" funny. We have had plenty of the "ironic" variety of funny in our lives. Again, perspective is everything. It's how you decide to process the information once it's provided you.

Jessica was able to learn new strategies to process the information given to her. Sometimes it had to be given to her in reverse order. At other times it meant simply redirecting the attention away from what could have been an uncomfortable situation; for example, if we had seen something that might have upset her on the side of the highway and I could use the exercise to distract her, then it was a great tool. At other times, it was used to deflect the attention away from the fact that we weren't doing anything particularly interesting so that Averie would not whine about being bored. He's learning. Jessica got those lessons early. I'm still working on it with Averie but he's getting it.

At all times, it took a commitment to the goal, and a lot of patience – an interest in space travel, world folklore, molecular biology and elephants helps, too.

CHAPTER THIRTEEN

Household Chores

"Cooking the Laundry and Mopping the Dishes"

L earning to process information is important. In the last chapter we discussed how Jessica and I developed strategies to take the input that she received and learn to deal with it effectively. It is not always as simple as it might sound.

To help you understand our story more effectively, I need to give you the next part of our journey. When we left Japan, Jessica and I returned to my native state of Arkansas. It was time for Jessica to enter junior high school, and I was pursuing a doctorate in behavioral science. It was at this time that we met the Summers guys. Steve is a flight engineer for the Air Force, and was the custodial single father for his two boys, Alex and Averie. Averie has Autism. We soon became like the Brady Bunch, and Jessica found that she enjoyed having siblings. Steve and I married before Christmas of 2002, and he adopted Jessica shortly thereafter.

In previous chapters, I have made comparisons to computers and to computer people. A basic computer program is a series of simple commands in a very specific order. If the order is interrupted, the program will terminate, or end abruptly. The program may be interrupted by any number of things: the commands may be presented in the wrong order, there may be an electrical short in the computer system, there could be a problem with memory. Perhaps the program does not work in cooperation with other programs currently operating, and shuts the system down. Perhaps there is a "virus" in the system.

Processing information for the Autistic mind is very much like a simple program in a computer system; it works very delicately sometimes.

For many Autistic persons, things must be done in a specific order. Jessica learned to brush her teeth using a simple set of instructions in a simple order. It was not easy to accomplish, however.

At 4 years of age, I had to hold Jessica's head and brush her teeth for her while she bucked, fought and screeched. After I initiated the chaos regimen, she slowly began to understand that there were many ways that she could begin to help herself. I began by insisting that she go into the bathroom with me when I brushed my teeth, each day at a different time, and I explained the steps for brushing. Sometimes we brushed her teeth and sometimes we didn't. Chaos … you get the idea. Jessica never knew what to expect.

Gradually, Jessica would learn the steps to brushing and be able to do her teeth herself. It was a tremendous milestone for both of us. I called everyone I knew and told them about it within earshot of Jessica, so that she could hear the pride in my voice as I bragged about her accomplishment. I also encouraged Jessica to show off her grin, and commented on her pretty smile. Granted, at that time in her life, it was still a distant smile, pretty much vacant behind the eyes.

As she practiced her brushing technique, I observed her closely. It was at times like these that I became aware of how much like a computer program and an operating system the Autistic mind can be. Some small distraction can be like a "short in the electrical system," diverting all the energy from what has to be happening. Whereas I might be able to stop brushing my teeth to answer the telephone, and then finish the task after hanging up, many people on the Autism Spectrum cannot do that. A loud noise could distract Jessica from her task, and getting her back to the task would often take starting at the beginning. This is very similar to having to reboot the computer because it locked up after a "short" in the system.

Another common problem with Jessica's system was that the task at hand (the program currently running) "did not cooperate with other programs that were also running." This refers to Jessica's inability to change tasks easily, or to handle more than one thing at a time. Many Autistic people have difficulty in this area. If Jessica was engaged in her play, it would be extremely difficult to convince her that she needed to get up and go with me to brush her teeth. Sometimes a statement like "Barbie needed to brush" would help get Jessica to the bathroom.

It would be an interesting discussion, however, since most of her Barbies had no teeth. At times we might go "hunting for birds" in the bathroom, and not finding any, we would take a minute to brush before going back into her room. Chaos dictated that it not become part of a bedtime ritual, so it wasn't.

When I mentioned "memory" at the beginning of this chapter, it was a play on the double meaning of the word. Stored memory or available memory in the hard drive of a computer is much different from the memory the mind draws upon when processing information given naturally. Memory problems in Jessica's case were due to her simply forgetting how to do things after they had been explained to her. You might say that the operator had forgotten to "save" the information to Jessica's disk.

Simple, everyday tasks became our goals. They were, after all, what I envisioned Jessica would want to be able to do by herself one day. So I got busy teaching Jessica practical things. When building a regimen, you can decide to teach shapes and colors, for example, or you can teach life skills. It takes an enormous amount of patience, but I came to the realization early on that I could spend my time teaching Jessica to sort colored blocks and laugh with her about it, or I could spend my time teaching her to sort laundry and laugh with her about it. I chose the latter, and at the end of that time together, she would not only know how to sort colors, she would also know how to do laundry.

Jessica learned to cook. We cut vegetables into shapes together. We talked about nutrition and meal balancing. She learned how to make simple meals. At first, she was only allowed to use the microwave, but she has been using the stove since age 10. As she grew older, her responsibilities increased. She learned to do dishes. She learned to take care of the family pets. She learned to mop the floors. Now, like any other teenager, Jessica dreads her chores. However, she does them daily and earns a weekly allowance. She can also care for younger children.

"Cooking the laundry and mopping the dishes" is a phrase that I coined out of sheer frustration. As I reread the passages that I have written, it all seems like it fell into place easily. I cannot emphasize strongly enough that a wealth of patience is required for any regimen you undertake with a child with Autism. Jessica and I did not have a road full of only successes. We encountered many things along the way that did not work.

I mentioned earlier that Jessica never learned to ride a bicycle. It wasn't for lack of trying. When I bought a tricycle for her, she pushed it in circles in her room. She never allowed it to be taken outside. Because we were working on other areas of her therapy and I was picking my battles carefully, I didn't push this issue. When she outgrew the tricycle, I bought her a small bicycle with training wheels, and kept it on the enclosed porch of our house. I would take her outside and make several attempts to get her on the bike. She would allow herself to be pushed on the bike, but would never pedal it with her own feet. At long last she found a way to have fun with the bicycle outside – she would push it over and spin the wheels and watch the spokes as the sunlight danced off the spokes!

When we moved, we had a yard sale, and I sold the bicycle. I concentrated on other areas of Jessica's therapy. It was two years later, when Jessica was 9 years old, that she finally learned to balance on two wheels. This was accomplished on a scooter given to her by her great-grandmother, my MeeMaw. Soon, Jessica could be seen whizzing down the sidewalks in Japan on her scooter. However, she was the only one with a scooter. All of her friends had bicycles. She still could not ride a bicycle.

Again, perception is the key. I chose to view our failures as opportunities to eliminate some technique that did not work. People often talk about running into brick walls. We all "hit the wall" sometimes. I perceive the wall as made of glass, and in my mind, I can see beyond it to another option. "Maybe there is another way to explain it. Maybe there is another opportunity to teach it. Maybe it will work next time, in another location." I had to keep trying. I had to be prepared to hit the wall. In fact, I had to anticipate the wall at all times.

Nevertheless, hitting the wall will frustrate you. The tragic beauty of Autism is that the same person often is capable of doing extraordinary things very well, while being unable to perform simple tasks with reliability. For example, there are tales of Autistic savants who have no concept of how to keep themselves clean, or groom themselves, and yet they can meticulously groom and maintain some unbelievably complicated and magnificent masterpieces in art, music, architecture, landscaping, or a beautifully choreographed chess strategy. Any discipline will do. The point is that the attention to detail in every facet of the life of the person with Autism may be grossly uneven.

New skills for Jessica were taught one by one. But first each skill was broken down to a basic list of steps. Remember the example of the egg, and the thinking going from A to B to C to D to E? Teaching Jessica to mop the floor takes a number of steps. There are many more steps than you might imagine. The first time I show her visually because Jessica is a visual learner, but after that, I give her a list of verbal instructions. Something like this:

1. Go to the hall closet.

2. Open the door.

3. In the bottom of the closet is a bucket. Get that bucket.

4. Close the closet door.

5. Take the bucket into the kitchen.

6. Put it in the sink and turn on the water.

7. Put warm water into the bucket until the bucket is half full of water.

8. Turn off the water.

9. Now, open the cabinet under the sink and get the bottle of cleaner. Unscrew the top of the bottle of cleaner.

10. Use the blue cup (attached to the cleaner bottle) to measure some cleaner and add it to the water in the bucket.

11. Rinse the cup out with water.

12. Screw the top back onto the top of the cleaner bottle.

13. Put the cleaner and the cup back under the sink and close the cabinet.

14. Now your water is ready to mop.

It seems like a long list to do something as simple as mopping the floor – and Jessica hasn't even touched the mop yet. A list like this is broken down into steps of two or three instructions at a time. Jessica's mind could not make the connection from one step to the next in any logical progression. It became rote memorization after a while. If she were distracted and happened to skip a step, it did not take long to discover it. For instance, it would not be unreasonable to believe that she would forget to turn off the water, and leave it running for hours.

After the above lesson, Jessica does not leave the water on any more. She does not skip this step. It is because she has gained an understanding of water conservation. Jessica understands that we have a water bill to pay, and that being a responsible person means that you use only what you need. It takes a little longer to do that level of explanation, but it is a more progressive form of therapy. There is a deeper level of consciousness to her thinking as she is mopping the floor. She is learning to think about many different things simultaneously, instead of in the same repetitive patterns.

Many people talk about behavioral modification turning individuals with Autism into "robots." The therapy seeks to teach a behavior, and never explains the need fully. It seemed to me that without a solid understanding of why she needed to turn the water off, perhaps she wouldn't do it. She had demonstrated the ability to apply common sense once it was taught to her. She understood "if" and "then." It was time to really tackle "why" and "because."

As mentioned earlier, with nearly every new technique, I started with a discussion. Jessica and I would talk about what we would be doing, and how we would be doing it. I did not simply want her to stop behaving in a certain way. I wanted her to understand fully the need behind a given lesson. Then, I was sure she would want to change the behavior for all the right reasons.

When using visual demonstrations, usually, once was enough for Jessica to learn any lesson, as in the above case of mopping the floor. Understanding the reasons behind doing what she did was the key element in her doing them correctly. She turns off the lights to conserve energy because we talked about the importance of not being wasteful. She often picks up trash because she has an understanding about environmental issues.

When working with a person on the Autism Spectrum, like Jessica, it is important to remember that you can never take for granted that the lesson they have just learned will spread into other areas. For instance, a child who learns not to play with his food at home may play with his food at school because he has not applied the lesson outside the environment in which it was learned. Jessica thought that the only kind of mop that was suitable to use was the kind that we had at our house. In the house wares department of the store, she was surprised to see so many different kinds of mops.

"Do these all work?" she asks.

"Of course they do," I reply. "People get to choose which they like the best."

She points at a mop identical to ours. "That's the best mop," she says. "The rest don't work."

"Have you tried any of the rest of them?" I ask her.

She shakes her head. "No."

"Then how do you know?" I ask.

She frowns at the mops and looks thoughtful.

"Do you remember when you didn't want to go on Splash Mountain at Disney World because you thought that it would be scary?" I say.

We had visited Disney World when Jessica was 7 years old, and I had insisted that she go on several rides despite her efforts to convince me otherwise. Jessica had screamed and cried and tried to drag me away from the entrance to the Splash Mountain ride. But after she tried it, we waited in line another hour so she could ride it again because she loved it.

"Splash Mountain is so cool. I didn't know it would be cool," she says.

"Well, sometimes you have to do things, or at least you have to try things. You shouldn't decide that one thing is the best and all the rest are bad. If those mops didn't work at all, they wouldn't be for sale." I say.

"Yeah, I guess so. Hey, Mom, can we go to Disney World this summer?"

With every new task, as with every new thinking process, it would take a lot of explanation. Learning to mop the floor was a therapy project. It took a long time. It would have been easier to do it myself. Frankly, the floor had to be remopped for a long, long time. But she was learning, and it was about her learning.

She was learning about the need to live in a clean environment. She was learning to trade chores with her brothers, favor for favor, and be part of a team. She was learning to gain an appreciation of taking care of the place where you live. She gradually became better at mopping, and gets better at other things, too.

I wondered about the benefits of teaching her to think like everyone else. After all, psychotherapists could easily run the world because many people have a problem with thinking for themselves. Jessica will be much better equipped to deal with the world around her if she understands how others around her are processing information. Helping her to think in these ways are preparatory skills, much like teaching her to eat with a fork and spoon instead of with her fingers.

There are always bumps in the road, where the lines of communication are crossed, and you end up "mopping the dishes." There are times when Jessica is not paying attention, or is very tired, and we have difficulty. It is at times like this that she becomes very literal. Then I have to give her specific directions, or she will not understand what she is supposed to do.

At times like this, we also take the opportunity to laugh. Humor is very important in our lives. I have touched on it several times before, but here is an excellent opportunity to highlight how we laugh at ourselves. I often encourage Jessica to laugh at herself because it is healthy. Humor is elusive to many Autistic people. I thought that instilling a healthy sense of humor in Jessica was of great importance.

An example of humor was one afternoon after Jessica had arrived home from school. She got off the bus, and came in carrying her backpack and art portfolio. She went directly to her room to drop it off. In a few minutes, Jessica came to me at the computer, where I was doing some research on the Internet.

"Mom, whatcha up to?" She asks.

"mfphlrx …" I murmur something incoherent about research.

"What was that again?" She asks, wide-eyed now.

"Sorry. I'm researching some stuff. How was school? Got any homework? Tell me the scoop," I say, not looking up from the screen.

She launches into her tales of the day. They include what she's discussing in literature class, the girls' gossip from her lunch table, and which guy she has a crush on. It's pretty much a typical day at Mills High School.

"Okay, get on your chores," I say.

"I know, Mom," she says, rolling her eyes. She has emphasized the word "know" like every other teenager in the world. It makes me smile. It's music to my ears.

I think about the chore list for the day, broken into three sections for the three children in our family. I know that today Jessica must mop, and she's on kitchen help. Kitchen help means that she unloads the clean dishes from the dishwasher and prepares to load the dirty ones. I decide to give her a gentle reminder, because it's what moms do.

I call over my shoulder, "Today, Jessica, you're on mopping and dishes."

Her face screws into a look of utter confusion. "Mopping the dishes?"

"No." I say. "Mopping and also dishes, as in 'you have to mop and then you are on kitchen help.'"

"Mopping and dishes," Jessica says.

"Yes."

"What do I mop?" she asks.

"What do you mop?" I ask.

We look at each other. It dawns on me that she does not know. The misunderstanding over mopping the dishes blew her mind. It strikes me as hilarious.

"The ceiling," I say finally.

Jessica's eyes go wide. She looks at the ceiling. "The CEILING??"

I look at her, nod my head and use an imaginary mop to show her what mopping the ceiling would look like. Then I look at her and grin.

"You're joking," she says, finally.

By this time I am nearly doubled over with laughter. We laugh at my pantomime of mopping the ceiling for a few minutes, and then I go back to research and she gets to mopping … the floor.

I tell Jessica that it is important not to take herself too seriously, and not to take others too seriously either. Laughter is important. We find something to laugh about with amazing regularity. It is often at ourselves. Jessica has come to the conclusion that I am weird. Since most teens think their parents are a little strange, I won't worry too much about that. Besides, she is probably right.

CHAPTER FOURTEEN

Self-Esteem

"Do You Need the 'Jessica Lecture'?"

Building your child's self-esteem is a delicate matter, whether you are dealing with Autism or not. Every parent knows what I am talking about. Your child comes home from school and tells you that she has been the target of a cruel joke, or has been picked on by a bigger child; she is dejected. Perhaps your first instinct is to jump to the rescue. How dare somebody pick on your child!

We have all been there. In fact, most of us have been the target of such behavior at one time or another. But the person on the Autism Spectrum walks around with a target on his or her back at all times. If one child was to be singled out in the game, to have berries thrown at her, that child would have been my Jessica. It was heartbreaking.

In elementary school, it was impossible for her to understand why others were constantly mean to her. She was upset about the way she was treated at school every day. We had the same conversations over and over again. They came to be known as the "Jessica lectures."

One of our standard Jessica lectures is that it is impossible to control the way that others behave. This is something we must accept. Jessica has had to learn that she can only control how she behaves, and that this includes how she reacts to others' behavior.

This may seem to be oversimplified, but once it is a standard part of your vocabulary, it is easily called upon for reference. For example, when Jessica came home from first grade upset because of something that had happened at school, we called upon this reference. We would discuss what happened:

Me: "Jessica, honey, what's wrong? Are you hurt?"

Jessica: (sobbing) "Yes."

Me: "Where are you hurt?"

Jessica points to her stomach. I look for signs of injury and find none. There is nothing that needs a bandage except her wounded feelings, as I soon discover.

Me: "What happened?"

Jessica: "I went to time-out."

Me: "Okay … and then what?"

Jessica: "And then my stomach hurt."

Me: "Why did you go to time-out? Did you get in trouble?"

Jessica: "No. The big one did it."

Me: "The big what, honey? Is that a teacher or another kid? What did they do? Can you show me?"

As the drama unfolded over the next few minutes, I discovered that "the big one" was a kid in her class who was bullying smaller children by stomping towards them and startling them. Many kids thought it was funny. Kids on the Autism Spectrum generally do not find this kind of behavior funny, nor do they find it comforting. Jessica put herself in time-out as a means of protection. By going to the time-out corner, she was out of the line of fire, so to speak. However, she missed the morning play time as well. The whole incident had given her a stomachache.

Me: "Jessica, move your arms like this." I move my arms over my head in a funny way. It makes her smile. She mimics me. "See how you can control your arms? But you can't control my arms, can you?"

Jessica: (shaking her head) "No."

Me: "You can't control anybody but Jessica. You can't control that big boy at your school. You can't control what he does. You can only control yourself. If he behaves badly, you can't control that. You can only control your good behavior. See that?"

Jessica: "Jessica's a good girl."

Me: "You just keep being good. And if he keeps being bad, you tell a teacher about it. Don't let him make you go to time-out. He shouldn't do that. You ask him to please stop. If he doesn't, then tell the teacher that you asked him to stop. You can't control him. You just control you. Worry about controlling yourself. And don't let it bother you so much that your stomach hurts. Okay? I'm proud of you."

Jessica: "Okay."

As Jessica has matured, we have often called upon that same example of "move your arms Jessica – can you control anybody but yourself, Jessica?" and turned a frown into a smile on days when she thought that the sky was falling. She also knows that she has the choice of whether or not she will let something bother her to the point that it makes her stomach hurt.

Choosing whether or not to let something bother you is another Jessica lecture. I tell Jessica often that she has many choices to make. We choose to be angry, sad, or glad. We choose to be wherever we are in our lives. Jessica and I choose to work hard in her therapy, and she has made tremendous progress. We choose to be extremely happy about that fact.

I figured out long ago that life was all about the choices that we make. Too often, people fixate on being optimistic or bemoan being pessimistic. In my opinion, the glass half-full or half-empty metaphor is meaningless. I am neither optimistic nor pessimistic. I am a realist. The glass is simply twice as big as it needs to be.

Think about that. Take any situation that you find yourself in, and look at it realistically. Ask yourself, "What do I have?" In the above metaphor, you can celebrate that you have a little to drink, or you can bemoan that you only have so little. The situation in either case remains the same. You still have a glass twice as big as is required. So, do something about it. Act on it. Find a new glass.

Being optimistic or pessimistic is, in my opinion, a waste of time in either case. With Jessica's therapy I didn't have the luxury of a lot of extra time. As a realist, I recognize that I can choose how to react when things happen. Just because I am not an optimist does not mean that I do not have a sunny outlook. I expect that good things will happen. I also know that bad things will happen, and I am prepared for them.

Building Jessica's self-esteem is very much like preparing her for when negative things happen. She must be prepared to call on her emotional reserves, and to feel strong when negative things happen. It is natural for parents to want to shield their children from events and topics that seem hurtful, but sharing "secrets" with our children is one way to build strong bonds with them.

To build strong relationships we all have to feel needed by somebody else. When Jessica's feelings would be hurt by someone's behavior or comments at school, I would tell her a story of how my own feelings had been hurt when I was a child. Sharing moments from my past would bring us closer together. I told her my secrets, and how much these things had hurt, to show her that I understood. Then, I told her that we had to choose not to let these things bother us.

Jessica appreciated my telling her my secrets. We are blessed that we can be close to each other. I tell her often that I am happy that she is good at keeping secrets. I always promise not to tell her secrets, and she promises not to tell mine. Suddenly these things that seemed so humiliating at first don't seem to matter so much anymore.

Jessica also learned to improve her listening skills by trading stories like this. I have always stressed to her the importance of listening to other people. Part of building her self-esteem has entailed her learning to read the faces of the people around her. Many persons on the spectrum are not able to read the expressions of others in the room, or the faces of the person they are talking to and, therefore, are unable to gauge how to react. Failing to read expressions of boredom, for example, they find themselves talking endlessly about the same subject, even when the other person is obviously disinterested. Or worse, they misunderstand what is going on around them, and laugh at something not intended to be funny and soon find themselves on the outskirts of the social circle.

Jessica would listen to my stories. I encouraged her to ask questions, and we would talk about my story. Then she would tell her story and I would ask questions about her story. I was teaching her how to be a good listener and how to take turns; it was practice for being a good friend, which I think is important. She is very good at this, and she is a very good friend.

As any child will do, however, Jessica sometimes becomes extremely self-involved. It is not uncommon for children to assume that all things that happen in their world, or to the people in their world, happen as a direct result of something that they have done, or not done. For example, this is why children of divorced parents often blame themselves for the breakups, and why they feel that they can resolve the situations between their folks. To most kids, the world revolves around them entirely.

When Jessica becomes the center of the universe, she takes on the problems of the entire world. It is a little different than for the average child. Since she processes information a differently, she begins to believe that anyone having any sort of trouble is suffering because of something that she has done, or that there must be something that she can do to make it better. Jessica would feed every hungry person in the world, and she would end every world conflict single-handedly, if only she could.

Related to that, Jessica can be extremely sensitive. If someone speaks to her in a slightly indifferent manner, she is hurt. Immediately, she begins to wonder what she has done that has caused that person's distress. This reaction brings on the most popular of the Jessica lectures entitled: "It's not about you."

From the age of 7, Jessica and I had this lecture once or twice a week. Jessica has had to learn to accept that others have lives and problems that exist outside the world that she lives in, and that they have nothing to do with her. There is nothing that she can do about them. She is not to blame. "It's not about you," I instructed her, and told her to simply forgive people for being human and for having troubles. I told her to hope in her heart that things would get better for whomever she was concerned, and then choose not to let it bother her.

═☆

As Jessica learned to do more things on her own, her confidence grew. And as confidence grows, so does self-esteem. Jessica is able to take care of herself, to do many household chores, including cooking for herself. She is able to keep up with her schoolwork and remain organized at school, in a regular high school where she has many friends. She is active in her youth group at church, and she speaks and sings often in the community, and she volunteers her time for others. Most of all, she feels she has a duty to other kids who can benefit from her experience.

Her experience could easily have been different than it was. I initially refused to enroll her in public school because the district was going to require that she wear a helmet due to head banging. I wasn't going to allow that to happen if I could prevent it. We were able to prevent it, so she did not have the added social stigma of a helmet or headgear. The last year that she had an Autism resource teacher checking in on her, I insisted that the teacher not pull her from the classroom, and instead only look through the window of the mainstream classroom to make sure that she was doing well.

In my opinion, the less singling-out Jessica had to deal with, the better. I did as much of her therapy at home and away from her school as possible. We had speech therapy administered at school, but we applied for only the minimum amount of help, so Jessica was not removed from the regular classroom for too much time; in addition, I took her to outside speech therapy for supplemental help.

At the beginning of her elementary school years, when Jessica and I were dealing with school administrators, there were many who felt that she would be too much of a distraction in the general education classroom. Parents were having difficulty finding programs where their children on the Autism Spectrum could be fully mainstreamed. I was having the same problem. When administrators saw the word Autism, they would immediately go to the diagnosis sheets telling of Jessica's rocking and spinning, her tics and shrieking. They would then decide that Jessica would dramatically reduce the focus level of the other students in the class.

School administrators have been coming around in their ways of thinking since Jessica was diagnosed in 1994. With the introduction of the

Individuals with Disabilities Education Act of 1997, or IDEA, more educators became ready to take on inclusion issues. In 2004, the IDEA became the IDEIA, or the Individuals with Disabilities Education Improvement Act. Suffice to say it is a much easier battle today than it was 10 years ago.

As Jessica mastered various skills, and as her various tics and inappropriate behaviors decreased, it became my mission to ensure that she received the same level of education as everyone else. She had rights. If I didn't fight for her, it was apparent that nobody else would. So I fought, and I won, but it took a lot of fighting, and some begging at times, too. Nevertheless, it was worth it, and Jessica got to prove to everyone that she had what it took to make it.

Looking back on all she has achieved, Jessica and I are proud of how hard she has worked. I tell her how proud I am of her every time I think about it. Don't ever make light of the pride you take in your child's accomplishments – it goes a long, long way in that building process.

CHAPTER FIFTEEN

Making Friends

"Gotta Be One to Have One"

The title says it all, doesn't it? It seems like it would be so simple. You should be able to teach your child how to be a good friend, and then the friends should just come knocking at your door. If only it were like that.

For Jessica and me, the whole idea of having friends has always been a tender subject. Many are under the impression that persons on the Autism Spectrum are indifferent to others, sometimes to such an extent that they are unable to function in a normal relationship. This impression can place a strain on relationships, whether with a parent, a therapist or a teacher. But relationships are necessary in everyone's life.

Within these relationships, parents, and the teachers and professionals in the life of the person with Autism know the "quirky" little eccentricities about the person's behavior, and after a while may even find them endearing. These people take the time to adjust to these behaviors and to allow the Autistic person time to adjust to them as well. It takes time to build any relationship.

A "friend," however, is somewhat of an extraneous relationship. It is not "necessary" for the other person. Sometimes people who do not live with Autism do not understand what is going on and, therefore, do not take the time to build a friendship with an individual with Autism. It is easy to assume that a person on the Spectrum is incapable of understanding what is going on. Therefore, it is easy for them to turn away and to go on with their lives.

For as long as she has been able to speak her wishes to me, Jessica has wished for friends. It has been a heartbreaking situation until recently. At first, she wished that the characters in the stories she was writing would come to life and keep her company. She would ascribe to them all the qualities that she looked for in her friendships. They would protect her, and they would never call her ugly names like "retard" or "freak." They would never throw things at her in the lunchroom, but would compete to sit with her.

She would talk to me about the things that the other kids did to her at school. They threw things at her, and called her horrible names. I did the best that I could to try to console her. I confess that there were many times that I wondered how much more either of us could take of the torture that public school was for her. She came home with a broken heart, and Mommy couldn't always kiss that boo-boo and make it all better. I don't blame the teachers or the administration. They have their hands full, and they always did the best they could. But the kids were often horrible to her, so sending her off to school every day was like sending her to a prison of sorts. But I kept doing it. I knew deep down that dealing with the aftermath was a therapy in itself. She remains the strongest kid I have ever known, and she has taught me more lessons in bravery than any person should ever have to learn in one lifetime.

Most of us can conjure up images of the school bully. Take a moment to go there in your imagination now. Remember what it was like to be teased. Relive your worst moment of ridicule – the words or the actions of the bully in your second-grade class. Did a grimace just twist across your face? I thought so. I grimaced myself as I wrote this, remembering my own bully.

I was lucky in that I was strong enough, and popular enough, to make friends easily. I did not have many run-ins with bullies. However, I watched others who were not so lucky. I remember what it was like growing up. And I admit that the words that were said to me hurt for a long time, even though I had many friends. Such comments can affect your sense of self-worth for years.

The best that we can do is to prepare our kids for when this happens. Not for *if* it happens, but for *when* it happens. When Jessica came home from school brokenhearted, we talked about the things that were said to her. These things would break my heart, too. I asked her to imagine the ugly things said as if they could be put into her pocket instead of being kept in her mind or in her heart. In this way, she might be able to continue to focus on her schoolwork instead of the social situation going wrong around her.

When she got home in the afternoon, we always discussed the events of the day. If there were ugly things to talk about, we would take them out of her pocket and go over all the reasons why the things that were said about her weren't true. Then we would get a note card and write down the ugly thing said on one side, and the truth on the other side. She was able to keep these cards to read later if she needed to remember the lesson.

Some of the lessons were very short, and some were sweet. Many of them were humorous. They all were fairly simple. Let me illustrate one lesson that we used fairly often.

As mentioned, I have always told Jessica stories from my childhood, and I often share stories of where I was embarrassed or humiliated. I try to find some reason to laugh at myself. If we laugh at me, then it's easier for her to laugh at herself, and then she lightens up and starts to take herself less seriously. One of my favorite stories involves a particularly nasty boy in my class who called me a geek. This boy had been merciless in his taunting of my friends and me over a number of years, and was only slightly less rude to teachers and administrators. He was a child of privilege, with wealthy parents who gave him everything that he wanted; he was bratty and spoiled. Those few who were in his circle of "friends" were as nasty as he was. I ignored all of them.

One day when he called me a geek, I viewed his comment as a compliment, considering the source. True to my somewhat nerdy nature, I smiled, raised one eyebrow, and asked him if he knew what a geek was. He said he didn't know, so I took the opportunity to educate him. I told him that a geek was a sideshow act, where a person would bite the heads off live chickens, and since he was an (insert the vernacular reference to a donkey here), he likely was in no danger. It was a great triumphant moment in my life. The look on his face was priceless, especially as he had his flunkies about him, and he'd just been busted by his prey. That group didn't pick on me after that, but instead tried to take me under wing. I resisted. By that time, I had a group of my own.

Jessica loves that story and asks me to tell it to her from time to time. Not surprisingly, one of the cards she used to carry said "It's okay to be a geek." It had a smiley face beneath the words.

I wrote that I considered the word "geek" to be complimentary, and I do. In the last few years there have been television shows, clothing styles, musical trends, indeed a whole genre has been dedicated to geekiness. I believe we are supposed to call it individuality. Call it what you want. I think it's all wonderful. Remove all the stigma associated with the words and embrace your geekiness.

This is emotional conditioning. The reason that I started with a word like that is that everyone can relate to a word like "geek." It's a short jump from "geek" to terms like "freak" or "weirdo." Conditioning someone to eat new foods, or to be able to process touch so that she can be held or hugged, is easier to understand because these examples are a part of physical conditioning. But words can hurt, and they stick for a long time if you let them.

It was important that Jessica had the right attitude going in. If you are able to laugh at yourself, you are more likely to be the sort of person who attracts friends. I showed Jessica how she was funny. It was amazing. She had been unaware of all the things that she did that were amusing. Humor is so elusive to the individual on the Spectrum. This is not to say that she always understood every joke all the time, but it gave her more practice in what most people thought was funny.

Jessica is funny, but not in the "class clown" sense. She is not the sort of kid who would ever disrupt a classroom purposely, even to send the students into gales of giggles. She would love to be a comedienne, I believe, but she is much better at telling other people's jokes than at coming up with her own. Nevertheless, watching comedy tapes has helped to fine tune her sense of humor and develop her "funny-ness."

Over the years, we have also practiced what I like to call "emotional savvy." Jessica and I spent a lot of time people watching. We would watch people walk, we noticed the way they moved, the way they held their purses, the way they looked at one another, the way they laughed, and the way they touched their hair. We studied the looks on their faces, and we talked about what they might be feeling. We talked about appropriate public actions and inappropriate public actions as part of making rules for how to behave in public. She got it. Jessica can maintain herself now, and feels so much more self-confident.

Jessica understands Autism, and she understood from an early age what Autism was doing to her brain. She understood why others would not see things as she would see them. This made it much easier for us to "decompress" when she was having an episode. We would go about it much like one might deal with an asthma attack. It happens, and you handle it. It's a biological thing you have to work to overcome. If you treat it like something debilitating, it becomes debilitating. Jessica hasn't had an episode in years. But she used to have them daily, and as described earlier, they were very bad when she had them.

Jessica remembers where she was, and has a strong memory of what it was like to be in a "dark place," in The Void. She knows how far she has come. She and I celebrate that journey daily, and we see it as an ongoing process. It is wonderful to see her take pride in the person she is today, and in the person she is becoming.

Who she is becoming is somebody really wonderful, and I am not the only person to recognize and appreciate it. She has been blessed with friends this year. It was heartbreaking to watch her remain friendless for so many years. She was the loneliest child I knew. She wanted friends more than anyone in the world. I tried everything I could. I arranged play groups, I had sleepovers, bowling parties and makeover parties and did all the "cool" things that could be done for preteens. Still, few good friendships came out of it – until high school.

High school brought about a maturity in Jessica, and a maturity in the other kids, that was lacking in past years. The acceptance into a circle of friends makes a big difference in the life of a child. Jessica's sense of self-esteem improved dramatically as she collected friends. She is a good friend to have. She is kind, caring, compassionate, funny, and extremely loyal.

As her mother, I believe that I am most proud of her taking an interest in others who share our journey. When we began this book project, Jessica and I were being asked to speak and sing at events, and share our story. Jessica wanted most to speak to other kids with Autism, to tell them herself to not be afraid to try new therapies. She said that she remembered being afraid because the therapy would be different and new, but that now her life was so much better. "They need to know, Mom." She said. "I could tell them."

And who better to tell them than one who knows?

"IS THERE A CURE FOR NORMAL?"

Children are the cruelest punishers to each other:
pointing out the slightest flaws, one from another,

focusing on each person and making it some sick game,
to make each one unsure of whether they should like their name.

Your hair, your clothes, the way you speak, is all under the glass.
Unless you're in the popular group, you're likely not to pass.

If you're on the Autistic Spectrum, you've given them extra cause,
but is there a cure for normal? Boy, I sure wish there was!

My Spectrum kid just wanted to be friends with the other girls.
She showed up dressed like all the rest, blonde hair a mass of curls.

She didn't get the joke, and so the next one was on her.
They ran screaming from her at recess. They really caused a stir.

She came to me, lips quivering, as parents came that afternoon.
She couldn't say what happened or ask if we were leaving soon.

She hugged her knees and rocked as they went racing to the car.
I said "those kids are normal and that's just the way they are."

They soon found out that they could make her part of lots of fun
and get her into trouble at the same time: they would run,

then call her name and say "come play with us!" and when she came,
happily running up to join her "friends" to play a game,

they would tell the teacher she was running, against a classroom rule,
and she would be sent to sit on the bench next to the school.

She could not tell the teacher what the normal kids had done.
She had to sit and watch them laugh. They thought that this was fun.

My Spectrum kid was the sweetest girl of any in her grade.
She's eaten dirt for some of them, and others she has paid.

Some convinced her to wait in the lunchline and pay double.
Others taught her nasty words to get her into trouble.

She's done their work, or given gifts, and worried herself sick
that being friends with people takes some special sort of trick.

She wanted only for a friend, a best friend, to be true
and couldn't understand that this was difficult to do.

My Spectrum kid came home one day, her face dragging the floor,
her spirits lower than I think I'd ever seen before.

She needed me to tell her what "gimp" and "freak" meant.
The kids at school were giving her new nicknames with intent.

I told her to dismiss those things they said to her that day.
"They're normal so you shouldn't put your trust in what they say."

She asked me if I wanted her to be a "normal" girl.
"No," I said. "but I want a normal life for you in the world."

"I want for you to go to school like normal children do,
and learn to drive and go on dates, and deal with heartbreak, too.

I want to see you strive and fail and strive again and win.
I don't mind answering your questions time and time again.

I want the same chances available so that you can choose.
It's not important if you win first prize or if you lose,

as long as you are able to live your life like all the rest
and you're given the opportunity to always do your best."

While some things may be more challenging at times for her than most,
she has many gifts and talents about which she could boast.

If she were normal, you might hear her boasting right out loud!
She doesn't, so it's just another reason why I'm proud.

We're closer than normal moms and daughters are to one another,
We've a journey shared between us far surpassing child and mother.

If I could change my Spectrum kid, I simply wouldn't do it.
She's perfect just the way she is. That's all there is to it!

Conclusion

"You Can't Argue With Results"

Not surprisingly, over the years I have had to go head-to-head with clinicians who were concerned that I didn't have a set routine for Jessica. "What? You don't have a routine at home?" they would exclaim and then listen to the chaos explanation. Many were converted. Some shook their heads and went back to their traditional way of doing things. Many of these people were like those old oak trees that were inflexible, and ended up splintered on the street after Hurricane Fran. "This is the only way to do it …" is perhaps the greatest way to be inflexible, and the quickest way to be blown down in a storm.

Without exception, though, they were impressed with Jessica's progress. At the beginning it was suggested that the good results were due to the fact that I was Jessica's mother, and because I was good at working with my child. I was sure this was not the case and then began giving the regimen to other parents to use with their children. It works for others, too.

One child whose parents I began corresponding with in Tennessee wrote that as a result of implementing a regimen of chaos, they were able to live a more "regular" life. Their son was in junior high school and had not been able to join his classmates on any school trips because of behavioral outbursts. This was the reason they had contacted me. I helped them to lay out a schedule of chaos to attend to that one area in his school life.

Soon he was able to go on the trips. In addition, he was soon able to advocate for himself in other areas. He educated many of his peers about Autism and how it affected him, and helped them distinguish Autism from mental retardation. He gained the respect of his peers and his teachers, and learned ways to control his behavioral outbursts to such a degree that the school counselor invited him to join an after-school club. His self-esteem grew, his grades improved, and his parents were thrilled. As a result, other areas of his school life, and then his home life, also gradually improved. The relationship with his parents improved. Out of this came willingness from his father, and then a neighbor, to volunteer at the young man's school. The three of them now work together to teach younger children to read. It is incredible how the one small change (being able to go on school trips) has affected a much greater change in this young man's life? All these changes took place in the span of eight months.

Another more dramatic change as a result of using a regimen that incorporates chaos theory is illustrated by a young man aged 18. Nothing much has ever been expected of him. Most of his teachers do not understand Autism well. One of his teachers wrote to me, explaining that he had been "lost in the system." She was taking the place of his paraprofessional in the school. With permission of his parents and the special education teacher, she sent me a copy of his latest IEP, and I laid out a schedule of chaos for him. Within two weeks, he was responding in dramatic ways. He was listening and attempting to do the work, and with some modification and flash cards, was doing as well in one class as every other student in the class. It is important to note that this young man falls between the moderate and severe range on the spectrum, and although he is verbal, he displays some fairly complex behavioral tendencies such as squealing and flapping. Nevertheless, he is on board with his parapro, willing to try to handle some of these behavioral issues at his own pace.

As stated early on, I recognize that the regimen described here will not work for everyone, any more than one form of chemotherapy will work for every form of cancer. However, it's a viable option. Here it is. Here is our story. Here is our success. Let me add something: The experts are always insisting that early intervention is the key to turning the tables on Autism. Let me tell you about Averie, my stepson.

I have been in Averie's life for just over four years. He was diagnosed at age 4 with mild to moderate Autism. When I met Averie, he was 8 years old. He was unable to sleep in a room without his brother, and he suffered from night terrors. To get ready for bed, he would have to be instructed through his nightly routine, and he sucked his thumb. He was echolalic, and had a prominent stutter. He was in resource classes in school, and could barely read. He was in second grade, but was being given kindergarten-level work to complete in the resource class. He made very little eye contact. He was terrified of the sky, and frequently cried when leaving for school, or when leaving school to return home because he thought that there would be a storm. Averie's food repertoire consisted of nine foods, in three different color groupings. This is even a generous list, as it includes two brands of hot dogs, and two varieties of chicken. It made eating out difficult, if not impossible.

Averie will soon be 12. His stutter is gone, and the eye contact is nearly flawless by what you might consider "normal" standards. He can be told to take a shower and get ready for bed, and he is able to do all that needs to be done by himself. This is miraculous when compared to three years ago. I designed and built a Snoezelen-like habitat (see Glossary) in the front room of our house as a transition room for him; it worked wonders. He has his own room now, and sleeps in his own bed. He hasn't had a night terror in over a year. He slept with a night-light, but when it burned out, he was fine without it. He does chores, and even operates the vacuum cleaner in his bedroom. He takes care of the family dog. He's taking Tae Kwon Do, and will soon test for his advanced red belt. Last year he rode his bike to and from school, or walked. This year, he takes the bus with his brother and sister to the junior high school. He can cook simple meals. He earns an allowance – when he doesn't do his chores, he doesn't get his allowance. He participates in youth group events at church, and has speaking parts. He is a brave and responsible young man with a good sense of humor and a strong sense of consideration for the feelings of other's. He rode the bus to church camp this summer and stayed for four nights away from home and made lots of friends.

This spring he participated in the science fair for the second year in a row. Three years ago, he was in a resource class, barely able to read. His resource class would have been marched through the fair to look at the projects. This year, he is mainstreamed into all his classes. His science project was more difficult than the majority of those in his class, and he worked very hard. When we went to the fair, the teachers and students were impressed with his project. He was very proud of it, and has already been thinking of how to improve it for next year. When people asked him about it, he was able to explain his project and talk about it. It was a night of triumph. It didn't matter who took home the blue ribbon. Averie won the fair, in my estimation.

But this isn't the end. Averie is now in Advanced Placement classes at his school, and after being on the honor roll at his elementary school for two years in general education classes, was chosen for the National Junior Beta Club, where he attended regular meeting and held an elected office as secretary/treasurer. He was also an Ambassador for his fifth-grade class, and gave tours around the school to visitors. Think about that! A child who was so unsure of his communication skills previously that he could not make eye contact, stuttered and sucked his thumb, was now selected by his peers to be an Ambassador and give tours to visitors. He did well. In addition to this honor, he ran for and won a position on the student council. At his fifth-grade graduation ceremony, he was awarded a citation and pin for Good Citizenship, one of only six given to students in the entire grade. While he continues to struggle with writing skills, he wrote an essay at the end of the year about ways to stay safe over the summer that won the essay competition. He was awarded a medal. He is aspiring to sing, and has a beautiful voice. This summer, he participated in the Air Force Family Talent Show, and sang a solo on the stage. The boy has guts. (I have been accused from time to time of being a "rooster mother" about my children – constantly crowing with pride about them. But truthfully, these guys give me plenty of reasons. They work hard.)

Averie's example alone is the end to the argument that early intervention is the only way to go. Don't ever give up. It is never too late! Continue to work because there is always a way to improve if you want to improve. I shudder to think where Jessica and I would be today if I had listened to some of the people who suggested I stop doing what I was doing to try to improve her situation.

I refused to give up on Jessica. I knew that if I kept going, I could make some headway. The people who held my hands along the way can attest to the fact that I claimed to be the most stubborn person alive. And tested me! Over and over again.

≡☆

In talking to both professionals and parents, I hear different viewpoints. One group within the Autistic community thinks that nothing should be done to change the individual with Autism. The mindset is that the person is Autistic and that we should allow her to be Autistic; we should embrace her Autistic-ness. The same group gets angry when you talk about finding a "cure" for Autism, listing dozens of brilliant people whose contributions we would surely miss if someone had "cured" them of their Autism.

And then there are others who think that you should do whatever you can to make your child "normal." This is what some people think I am trying to do with my children. I have been yelled at, admonished, and scolded for "recovering" my children instead of sitting at home wailing and collecting Social Security checks for them.

I don't think Autism needs a cure. Autism makes my kids who they are. It allows them extraordinary gifts and talents. It also brings challenges. I am merely attempting to give them all possible opportunities available to them. I am opening doors to them that would otherwise have been closed. I am showing them options. I have never said that Autism was a bad thing. I have never made my daughter feel embarrassed about who she is, because there is no reason to. I am enormously proud of all she has accomplished. I feel that she is perfect the way that she was created.

Jessica asked me once if I wanted her to be "normal." I told her that I did not. I wanted her to be better than most so-called normal persons. I was raising an extraordinary person, who would help others, and be honest and caring and considerate and kind. I wanted her to share and smile and know what it was like to love. My children, all three, are beautiful and perfect just the way they are made. Two of them happen to have Autism. I will do whatever I can to help them live productive lives with Autism.

The neurotypical (non-Autistic) middle child, Alex, is a gifted musician. He plays the electric guitar and is a bit of a daredevil on a skateboard. Sometimes it is tough on him to live with two siblings on the spectrum, but he is a great guy. He is given the same sort of disciplinary attention that the other two receive. Household chores are also evenly divided, and he's a great brother inasmuch as he knows when he needs to pick up some slack for the others and keep some of the pressure off mom and dad. Alex has had to grow up quickly, and is unbe-lievably mature for his age. He's awesome, and we have great discussions. I am lucky to have him around!

My final thought about Autism is this: Autism IS a big deal, because it takes over your life. However, there are many reasons why Auties and their families should feel empowered by being on the spectrum. I do not think that Autism is a terrible thing. It is an explanation for sheer brilliance in some areas of intellectual development, and a cause to celebrate that. It is also an explanation for behavioral difficulties that can threaten to drive parents to the brink of insanity.

Understanding Autism is the key to harnessing the power of the Spectrum in your child and your family. There is nothing wrong with a child who has Autism. Incorporating a therapy regimen helps an individual with Autism much like putting on a pair of eyeglasses helps a person who is near-sighted. Being near-sighted is genetic, and the levels of sight ability range from mild to severe. Mild sufferers only need glasses when reading or working on a computer. Severe sufferers are nearly or totally blind, and may require surgery to restore sight.

If little Johnny were near-sighted, his parents would most likely take him to get glasses, and then would insist that he wear them. That would be the rule. Eventually, the child will become accustomed to wearing glasses because they are beneficial to the way he lives his life. The parents might need to help Johnny deal with some "4-eyes" taunting at school, but that's pretty minor stuff. Kids and parents both buck up and get over all that, because everyone realizes that wearing glasses is what needs to happen for Johnny to be successful, now and in the future.

Near-sightedness is nothing more than a condition where the eyes process information differently; in this example, visual information. Why is it any different when thinking about what needs to be done for a person with Autism in the way of therapy? My argument is that it shouldn't be any different. You determine what needs to be done, and then you stand firm on it because it's the right thing to do.

This was what was in my mind every time Jessica fought what I tried to do initially. I imagined that she was trying to fling off a pair of eyeglasses because she didn't like them. Insisting upon the therapy was a little like picking them up off the floor and handing them back to her, instructing her to put them back on. Dropping the therapy because she didn't like it would have been irresponsible on my part, to my way of thinking.

As parents, the end goal is for us to help provide our kids the tools for success. Some of us are lucky, and our kids pick up a lot of the lessons they need to learn about how to behave in a social setting from watching the world around them. And some of us are lucky, and our kids have to be taught every lesson tediously, over and over and over until they get it.

Either way, we are lucky to be parents, and our kids are lucky to have us.

My efforts to help Jessica, from the very beginning, were motivated by a desire to see her succeed in every way possible. I want to give her every possible advantage I can. If that means that we spend time practicing eye contact and speech patterns so that they seem regular to others, and feel regular to her, then so be it. In a future job interview situation, she would be better suited for anything she wanted to do if not hindered by behavioral traits that she could monitor or change. Something as simple as being able to look the interviewer in the face and smile can help change the outcome of an interview and make the difference in future salaries perhaps. It's all been about the goal of giving her that life with purpose that she can be proud of. But SHE has to live that life for herself. She is becoming her own person, with her own thoughts, values and ideas. She makes me proud, every day of my life, to be her mom. She is very groovy. Because she is her own groovy person, she deserves the very best that I can do for her to give her every opportunity, like everybody else.

In addition, being able to socialize better with others will enrich all parts of her life, at work and at play. Every possible advantage that she can have is one that I want her to have; therefore, our goals have always been high. She has risen to the challenge time and time again.

Finally, I would not change my daughter. She is perfect the way she is. I have always been proud to accept her as she is. I said earlier that perception is the key to happiness. I perceive that I am blessed with a great kid in Jessica. We are on a journey together; the road has been rocky at times, but I wouldn't trade it for anything in the world. We have learned a lot, laughed a lot, and loved a lot … and are looking forward to the future. Our perception is that the best is yet to come.

Glossary

Accommodation: In cognitive development, the feeling that every experience is a new one, regardless of how similar it is to any previous experiences.

Assimilation: The ability to change the environment to meet your needs. Experiences are accepted only when they fit into what is already known; that is to say, new ideas can only be processed by attempting to fit them into the old ideas. For instance, children learn to play soccer because they already know how to run and to kick a ball.

Auditory discrimination: The ability of the brain to separate sounds. When the brain cannot separate sounds, conversations are lost in the noise of the room, and it becomes nearly impossible to focus on important tasks. Outside noises, traffic, or background music can interfere with the ability to concentrate.

Auditory sensitivity: A disorder that can hinder the ability to process what a person hears. Certain sounds can be painful or confusing, and can limit the amount of enjoyment that persons have in certain activities, (e.g., fireworks). Sometimes these sensitivities must be accepted, while others may be handled with conditioning, or by adapting with earplugs.

Behavior modification therapy: Therapy that uses conditioning, biofeedback and reinforcement to significantly alter human behavior. In the past, aversive therapy or painful techniques have been used. I don't do this kind of therapy. There is a need for therapy, and it is sometimes uncomfortable, but this discomfort is because the sensory integration dysfunction is being pushed to the person on the Autism Spectrum's limit. I do not agree with causing physical pain. I do believe that stepping outside the "comfort zone" is necessary, however, if true progress in any therapy regime is going to be seen.

Bilateral coordination: The body's ability to use both sides at the same time. People on the Autism Spectrum often have difficulty in this area, and resort to long periods of inactivity. They can be seen walking without swinging their arms. They are likely to have difficulties also in fine-motor movement activities such as using a knife and fork, tying shoes, and writing. Gross-motor movement activities such as running, throwing a ball, dancing and hopping on one foot may be difficult as well. Poor reading skills are often associated with this lack of two-sided coordination.

Echolalia: Sometimes called "parroting" because of the ability a person displays in mimicking another voice or pattern of speech. Among persons on the Autism Spectrum, echolalia is most closely associated with repeating the last word or words in a spoken phrase … the last words in a spoken phrase … a spoken phrase … phrase … phrase … Depending on the verbal ability of the individual, the words do not always have meaning associated with them.

IEP (Individualized Education Program): A student's short- and long-term education goals agreed upon between administrators and the parents and the teachers, pursuant to the individual state's special education guidelines. Federal law states that a multidisciplinary team must determine whether or not a child has a disability and requires special education services. IDEA (the Individuals with Disabilities Education Act) requires that certain information be included in the IEP, but it doesn't set a certain standard for how the IEP should look. Therefore, IEPS can be very different from one state to another.

Neurotypical: Non-Autistic, or not known to fall within the autism spectrum.

Obsessive compulsive disorder: A distorted perception of reality that causes someone to obsess about a certain topic. Frequent topics include whether the door is locked or if a glass has been cleaned properly. Topics of this nature can launch persons to become extremely anxious and worried. Often they engage in routines to clean themselves or their surroundings, or to lock the doors, etc.; these routines can become time-consuming and socially limiting. It is my opinion that these exercises fall extremely close to spectrum disorders, and can be conditioned, especially as they interfere with typical daily living, and often cause anxiety to people, and make them feel embarrassed. There is no reason to feel embarrassed. Things that make you anxious cannot be helped. They must be understood to be overcome. If they cannot be overcome, they must be accepted.

Olfactory sensitivity: A disorder that can inhibit a person's ability to process odors and scents. Smells of all kinds can cause distress, and can cause nausea and vomiting in extreme cases. Because of this, it often becomes hard for persons on the Autism Spectrum to focus properly in strong-smelling environments.

Pedantic speech: Overly formal speech. Words are used with extremely literal meanings and interpretations. Verbal youth often sound "much too mature for their years."

Prosody: In speech, the vocal tone and quality that is often missed by those on the Autism Spectrum. It embodies the characteristic of spoken language that helps to give meaning to spoken words. People on the Autism Spectrum are often unable to work out the subtle meanings behind what someone has said, and are unable to express their thoughts, or be subtle themselves. The dramatic quality and inflection that is placed upon words is sometimes lost as well. For example, the phrase "Never in all my life have I been so insulted" might be taken literally to mean that the person who said it had never been insulted. Persons on the Autism Spectrum often misunderstand the wonderful world of melodrama, and ironically, sometimes find themselves caught up in the middle.

Sensory integration: The process by which the brain organizes sensory input so we can interact with our environment in a meaningful way. For example, sight and hearing work together in the "normal" classroom setting. That is, a student can see the information written on the board and hear the instructions as they are spoken by the teacher. If the senses are processing the information in a meaningful manner, the student may have the opportunity to learn the information as it is presented.

Sensory integration dysfunction: A noticeable inability to properly integrate sensory input. This is generally because of some neurological disorder or irregularity. Common problems associated with sensory integration dysfunction include panic attacks, headaches, and severe difficulties in learning.

Snoezelen: (pronounced "SNOOZE-a-lenn") First created as a leisure activity in the Netherlands by Ad Verheul and Jan Hulsegge. Snoezelen habitats were specially designed environments for the needs of children and adults with severe and extreme mentally handicaps. Sensory-stimulating images and objects are combined to produce calming and pleasant effects. Contemporary use of Snoezelen has been adapted to the learning environment and to the therapeutic setting, and is not limited to the severe or the profound. Anyone, anywhere may find benefits in Snoezelen, as the sense of well-being and satisfaction, and sheer joy that can be discovered in such an environment stimulates a sense of creativity in many people, while others find it very calming. The use of bubble tubes, light tubes, fiber optics, fountains, mirrors, music kits, mobiles, black lights and stars on the ceiling, aromatherapy kits, stress balls, wind chimes, or any such device, may be included as these provide a calm and peaceful way to interact with one's surroundings. "Snoezelen" is derived from two Dutch words meaning "to smell" and "to doze."

Stim: A self-stimulating behavior (flapping, rocking, spinning, etc.) designed to calm or de-stress.

Tactile sensitivity: A condition whereby the brain misunderstands the signals sent by the nerves under the surface of the skin. As a result, a person may react strongly to various sensations such as light and firm pressure, pain and temperature. Textures may also be irritating and may make it stressful to take part in normal activities such as shaking hands or washing their hair.

Ticking: Involuntary movements, (such as blinking and finger fluttering), or vocal utterances, (such as grunting or coughing). These "tics" can become habits, or can become uncontrollable. Many people on the Autism Spectrum find it difficult to control ticking, and become embarrassed, or find it difficult to focus if they try too hard to suppress their "tics."

Visual sensitivity: A disorder that affects the ability to process information gathered through the eyes. This can result in poor reading and writing skills, an inability to judge objects in space in relation to one another and disorientation in following directions and finding one's way.

Recommended Reading

On Autism and Asperger Syndrome:

Attwood, T. (1998). *Asperger's syndrome: A guide for parents and professionals.* London: Jessica Kinsgley Publishers.

Cohen, S. (2002). *Targeting autism: What we know, don't know, and can do to help young children with autism and related disorders.* Berkeley: University of California Press.

Grandin, T. (1995). *Thinking in pictures and other reports from my life with autism.* New York: Doubleday.

Haddon, M. (2002). *The curious incident of the dog in the night-time: A novel.* New York: Doubleday.

Lovaas, I. (2002). *Teaching individuals with developmental delays: Basic intervention techniques.* Austin, TX: Pro-Ed.

Maurice, C. (1993). *Let me hear your voice: A family's triumph over autism.* New York: Fawcett-Columbine.

Myles, B. S., & Simpson, R. L. (2003). *Asperger syndrome: A guide for educators and parents.* Austin, TX: Pro-Ed.

Newport, J. (2004). *Your life is not a label: A guide to living fully with autism and asperger's syndrome for parents, professionals and you!* Arlington, TX: Future Horizons.

Ozonoff, S., Dawson, G., & McPartland, J. (2002). *A parent's guide to asperger syndrome & high-functioning autism: How to meet the challenges and help your child thrive.* New York: The Guilford Press.

Shore, S. M. (2003). *Beyond the wall: Personal experiences with autism and Asperger Syndrome.* Shawnee Mission, KS: Autism Asperger Publishing Company.

Shore, S. M. (Ed.). (2004). *Ask and tell: Self-advocacy and disclosure for people on the autism spectrum.* Shawnee Mission, KS: Autism Asperger Publishing Company.

Scott, J., Clark, C., & Brady, M. (2000). *Students with autism: Characteristics and instructions programming.* San Diego, CA: Singular Publishing Group.

Sicile-Kira, C. (2004). *Autism spectrum disorder: The complete guide to understanding autism, asperger's syndrome, pervasive developmental disorder, and other ASD's.* New York: Berkley Publishing Group.

Stone, F. (2004). *Autism – the eighth colour of the rainbow: Learn to speak autistic.* London: Jessica Kingsley Publishers.

Willey, L. H. (1999). *Pretending to be normal: Living with asperger's syndrome.* Philadelphia, PA: Jessica Kingsley Publishers.

For Kids:

Buron, K. D., & Curtis, M. (2004). *The incredible 5-point scale: Assisting students with autism spectrum disorders in understanding social interactions and controlling their emotional responses.* Shawnee Mission, KS: Autism Asperger Publishing Company.

Buron, K. D. (2004). *When my autism gets too big: A relaxation book for children with autism spectrum disorders.* Shawnee Mission, KS: Autism Asperger Publishing Company.

On Applied Behavior Analysis:

Cooper, J., Heron, T., & Heward, W. (1987). *Applied behavior analysis.* Upper Saddle River, NJ: Prentice Hall.

Gelfand, D. M., Jenson, W. R., & Clifford, J. D. (1988). *Understanding child behavior disorders: An introduction to child psychopathology.* Fort Worth, TX: Harcourt Brace.

Longres, J.F. (1990). *Understanding behavior in the social environment.* Itasca, IL: University of Wisconsin-Madison.

Newman, B. (2000). *Words from those who care: Further case studies of ABA with people with autism.* New York: Dove and Orca Press.

Newman, B. (2002). *Graduated applied behavior analysis.* New York: Dove and Orca Press.

Newman, B. (2002). *When everybody cares: Case studies of ABA with people with autism.* New York: Dove and Orca Press.

On Chaos Theory:

Gleick, J. (1998). *Chaos: Making a new science.* New York: Penguin Books.

On a Closely Related/Relevant Topic:

Hallowell, E. M., & Ratey, J. J. (2004). *Driven to distraction: Recognizing and coping with Attention Deficit Disorder from childhood through adulthood.* New York: Touchstone. (Eventually we will all come to the realization that ADD and ADHD are disorders that belong on the Spectrum. This is an argument that I have been making since 1996. It will most likely be another book, I suppose. We have an entire generation of injured kids. Pointing fingers at one another, bemoaning the situation and bringing the country to a standstill in the federal legal system may not fix things. We will have to first see that the glass is twice as big as is required. We will first have to recognize what we have, and then get going. If you do the cross-research for ADD/ADHD, you will see the bigger picture. The problem is larger than you realize ... much, much larger. This problem that we have in our country will be fixed in each individual home, one child at a time. You parents are the primaries – the most important caretakers and therapists, and you will make the difference in your children's lives, each and every day that you make the effort to give them lives with purpose. It matters.)

Appendix

A LETTER FROM LISA CRAVER

My name is Lisa Craver and I am honored that I have been asked to share with you. Currently, I am a Lead Psychologist with the Cumberland County School System in Fayetteville, North Carolina. I spend part of my time doing administrative and supervision tasks and the other half of my job consists of working with our special needs pre-school services. It was in that capacity that I first met Jessica in January 1994 when she was referred for evaluation.

At the time Jessica was seen for evaluation I was completing evaluations with an educational diagnostician and we went to see Jessica at her child care center. She presented as a pleasant little girl who did not make eye contact. Jessica did not appear to mind working with us as she sat at the table and did not attempt to get away, although Jessica was easily distracted. She was echolalic, repeating virtually everything that was said to her throughout the session. It was difficult to determine how much she really comprehended because of the echolalia. One thing in particular stands out in my memory from that time was that Jessica loved to count. If she ever got started counting it was very difficult to redirect her to something else. She counted perseveratively any chance she got. Jessica also pointed to and named the numerals on each page in the test materials. When she would get frustrated with attempts to redirect her she shrieked in a very high-pitched squeal. At times she would also hit herself in the head. Certainly, the first thoughts that came to my mind as I was evaluating Jessica were that she was autistic. Her behaviors were simply classic. I was convinced even more after speaking with Jessica's mother and hearing about Jessica's early history, which showed typical development to a point and then a loss of all her previously developed language skills.

The results of my evaluation were not encouraging, even though they were considered a minimal estimate of her cognitive skills due to her language difficulties. Jessica's performance on the Stanford-Binet, Form L-M, placed within the moderately mentally handicapped range (IQ - 50). Her mental development age was 2 years 2 months in comparison to her chronological age of 4 years 0 months. She appeared to be progressing in her cognitive skills at a rate approximately 50% that of her same-age peers. Jessica held her pencil in a fisted grasp and preferred to scribble in a circular fashion, although she did eventually imitate a vertical stroke after multiple attempts.

One of the recommendations as a result of my evaluation of Jessica was a referral to the TEACCH Center in Wilmington. Autism was still somewhat of a low-incidence handicap when Jessica was evaluated and we were not encouraged to make a diagnosis of autism at that time. The TEACCH centers were considered the premier agency in making that diagnosis. However, while Jessica was waiting for that evaluation to be scheduled, we were able to place her in a special needs preschool class in a typical elementary school which focused on language development every day. Jessica progressed well in that environment.

Lisa Craver, MA/CAS,
Lead psychologist, Cumberland County Schools
March 2005

AⱭPC

Autism Asperger Publishing Co.
P.O. Box 23173
Shawnee Mission, Kansas 66283-0173
www.asperger.net